To Tom.

Thanks for helping to make
Stand Up for Your Rights a
great success.
Paul Feldman 29/10/08

UNMASKING
THE STATE

a rough guide to real democracy

Action Guide No. 3

Paul Feldman

a world to win
for a future without global capitalism

Published by Lupus Books
PO Box 942
London SW1V 2AR

www.aworldtowin.net
info@aworldtowin.net
07871 745258

ISBN 978-0-9523454-5-9

Cover design Nick Feldman
Design and typography by Robbie Griffiths
Printed on FSC certified paper
Printed and bound by CPI Antony Rowe
Chippenham Wiltshire SN14 6LH

Contents

Introduction

Political discussion in Britain usually centres on what the government of the day is or is not doing and speculation about what might happen when a general election is called. Will New Labour lose to the Tories? Is David Cameron ready to become prime minister? Who knows and, frankly, who cares because this is politics as a trivial pursuit.

The narrowness of the debate is a reflection of the extremely limited nature of what is known as "representative democracy". This lynchpin of the capitalist political system serves many purposes. Principally, it focuses the electorate on the task of voting every four or five years for this or that representative, or MP. This is where you get a say in who will rule over you and your affairs – and that's as far as it goes in terms of political democracy. As someone once said, if voting changed anything they would make it illegal.

While the electorate is drawn into the politics of Tweedledum and Tweedledee, the rulers go on ruling and exercising power, whoever is in government. They command something more all-embracing than governments, which come and go. This is the state. Here we are talking about an array of inter-locking institutions and structures. This includes the machinery of government, the judicial system, the police and armed forces, quangos and executive agencies, the prison system and the monarchy. Together they constitute the modern state, a body that commands authority and has the power to enforce its decisions. No one really talks about the state, how it came to assume such tremendous power and what its primary purpose is. That is what this book sets out to do. It is called *Unmasking the State* for a reason. The core and the role of the state in Britain is disguised. This is accentuated by the absence of a written constitution and the popular prejudice that this is the natural order of things. Britain has a stable state while foreigners have turmoil and revolution.

Nothing could be further from the truth. The modern capitalist state was born in the Civil War of the 17th century, when Parliamentary forces defeated and then executed Charles I. As the book shows, those without power have contested the authority of the state since that time. The Levellers, the Radicals inspired by Tom Paine, the Chartists, Suffragettes and the mass unions have struggled against the state to establish political and social rights. Through the medium of representative democracy, ordinary people were able to build the Labour Party and use elections to defeat the Tory ruling class enemy for a few years at least. The fact that they can no longer do that is symptomatic of the changed times we are living through. Labour is now New Labour, and has been transformed into a party wedded to the capitalist market economy. A decade of New Labour has undermined the welfare state which, ironically, was established by Labour in the post-war period. Now we live in an authoritarian, market state where the vote counts for little and many millions are effectively disenfranchised.

The sharp decline of representative democracy as a political mechanism is truly the end of an historical era. What is posed now is not replacing New Labour with another parliamentary-based party but of finishing the unfinished business of the pioneering strugglers for democracy. This means going beyond the capitalist state and expanding democracy in new ways – into workplaces, public services, education and throughout the economy. This book is a contribution to that objective.

Paul Feldman
October 2008

1

The 'mystery' of the state

Most people understand what is meant by the term "government". This is made up of men and women who are said to *govern* the country. Yet the prime minister and ministers are part of a wider, much more significant body – the **state**. Governments come and go but the state itself not only lives on but evolves and adapts to new circumstances expressed through the actions of government.

So if you want to know how Britain is really *ruled*, as opposed to *governed*, you have to dig deeper, down into the recesses of the state. For the state is how and where real power – backed up by force and coercion – is exercised over people's lives. In Britain, the state is shrouded in mystery and mystique and appears as something natural, timeless and universal. So demystifying the state, bringing it out into the light of day, should help us answer some of the following questions in the course of this book:

▶ what is the relationship between the state and capitalism?
▶ how are the powers of the state exercised?
▶ are the powers of the state legitimately held? Can they be challenged?

- what is the relationship between democracy and the state?
- are the majority powerless or does the vote give ordinary people power?
- what rights, if any, do we have in relation to the state?
- is the modern state the last word on democracy?
- do we require new state forms to make a transition from a capitalist society to one based on co-operation and production for need?
- would change have to take a revolutionary form or can it be achieved through reform?

So what constitutes the state? The Chambers dictionary, for example, offers a variety of answers. One definition is that the state is a territory governed by a single political body. There is also reference to the "nation state" – which is described as an independent state with a population that broadly shares a common descent, language and culture. What concerns us here, however, is a further definition of the state as the **political entity of a nation** "including the government and all its apparatus, eg the civil service and the armed forces". In Britain, this also embraces the monarchy, Parliament, the judiciary, laws and the legal system, police and prisons, spy agencies MI5 and MI6, local government, a range of semi-government bodies and agencies and the established Church of England. Taken together, they constitute the modern British state. In turn, many national agencies now have global and regional relationships with bodies like the World Trade Organisation and the European Union, to which they have ceded substantial powers once reserved to the British state.

State bodies operate in a complex, often contradictory relationship with each other. Each branch of the state has its own particular history

Well concealed

The state is, then, in every sense of the word a triumph of concealment. It conceals the real history and relations of subjection behind an a-historical mask of legitimating illusion; contrives to deny the existence of connections and conflicts which would if recognised be incompatible with the claimed autonomy and integration of the state.

Philip Abrams, *Notes on the difficulty of studying the state*. Journal of Historical Sociology 1988 and development. This adds to the abstract, elusive nature of the concept of the state, particularly in Britain which is distinguished by the absence of a single, written constitutional document. Nevertheless, the general rules and regulations that govern the connections with each branch of the state are contained in a series of rules, regulations, precedents, conventions and laws that often operate in the background. For example, the fact that the victorious party at an election provides the prime minister, who in turn appoints members of the government without further reference to Parliament, is not explicitly stated in any document – but it happens.

A theory of the state

A study of these constitutional rules, precedents and conventions will tell us how the state operates on a day-to-day basis. But they will not in themselves reveal how the state came into being or what its overall social purpose and role is. What is important in this regard is to see the state in its interconnections with the rest of society, as a social, historically developing phenomenon. A World to Win's starting point is that the state has an objective existence. It exists independently of our consciousness and views about it. We may not recognise the state but the state certainly recognises us. Secondly, the state exists only in relationship to other parts of society. It can only be understood, for example, in its connection to economic relations, both national and global. In other words, the state is part of a greater whole. Thirdly, the state, as all other phenomena, has internal and external contradictions. For example, its role under capitalism limits its capacities and powers in relation to the economy. The need for popular approval and legitimacy is undermined by the state's alienated existence. Fourthly, the state is studied in its development, both in terms of its historic origins and how it is changing in the present.

A pioneering study into the origins of the state in society was made by Frederick Engels, the close collaborator of Karl Marx. In his *The Origin of the Family, Private Property and the State* (1884), Engels showed through an anthropological study of ancient, primitive societies – where no state existed – that the state was a product of society at a particular stage of historical development. This stage, he argued, marked the end of communal property and the beginning of private ownership.

Engels explained that the emergence of the state

> is the admission that this society has involved itself in insoluble self-contradiction and is cleft into irreconcilable antagonisms which it is powerless to exorcise. But in order that these antagonisms, classes with conflicting economic interests, shall not consume themselves and society in fruitless struggle, a power, apparently standing above society, has become necessary to moderate the conflict and keep it within the bounds of 'order'; and this power, arisen out of society, but placing itself above it and increasingly alienating itself from it, is the state.

Engels also argued that, as a rule, it is the "state of the most powerful, **economically dominant class**, which, through the medium of the state, becomes also the **politically dominant class**" [emphasis added]. So state power in any society has to be closely related to the dominant social classes in society. If it is not, then the state cannot function or establish legitimacy and authority and becomes vulnerable. Economic power in a class-based society requires political power for social stability and in order to reproduce, as well as develop, the best conditions for production. In this sense, the state represents a division of labour. Capitalists go on doing what they do best – producing commodities, exploiting labour and making profits. Politics is left to the state, to professional groups of administrators, politicians, civil servants, judges, prison officers, police and the armed forces. Capitalists are a diverse class with competing interests which is one crucial reason why they cannot rule directly. The state creates and then develops a framework within which the capitalist system of production is able to function.

In his preface to *A Contribution to the Critique of Political Economy*, Marx explained the relationship between the "political superstructure" and the "economic structure" of society. He described how political relations arise on the base of economic foundations and ultimately reflect the interests of the dominant class in society and that:

> In the social production of their life, human beings enter into definite relations that are indispensable and independent of their will, relations of production which correspond to a definite stage of development of their material productive forces. The sum total of these relations of production constitutes **the economic structure of society, the real**

foundation, *on* **which rises a legal and political superstructure** [emphasis added] and to which correspond definite forms of social consciousness. The mode of production of material life conditions the social, political and intellectual life process in general. It is not the consciousness of human beings that determines their being, but, on the contrary, their social being that determines their consciousness.

Over time, specialists in ruling like top civil servants, generals and judges have come to dominate affairs and have given the state a certain operational but relative autonomy. In this way, the state, rather than serving society, stands above and aloof from the population and is insulated from popular pressures. This adds to the impression that the existing state system is independent, neutral, normal and, above all, irreplaceable. This alienation is itself a reflection at a political level of the fact that people, both individually and socially, are deprived of the result of their own labour and the wealth produced by society as a whole.

While we are free to sell our labour power to an employer in return for a wage, once bought it becomes a good for use by the capitalist alone. The value added by labour belongs to – or is appropriated by – the employer and is the source of profit. Marx discovered that "this fact simply means that the object that labour produces, its product, stands opposed to it as something alien, as a power independent of the producer". He described this process as "a loss of reality for the worker, objectification as loss of and bondage to the object, and appropriation

A division of labour

State power is exercised through the state apparatus, or more precisely, through a system of state apparatuses. The separate existence of the state is part of a specific division of labour within society. Its internal organisation thus reflects in a particular way the social division of labour and the prevailing social class relations, contributing to their reproduction in the ever-ongoing social process. In the historical course of the class struggle, the state apparatuses come to crystallise determinate social relations and thus assume a material existence, efficacy and inertia which are to a certain extent independent of current state policies and class relations.

Göran Therborn, *What does the state do when it rules?* Verso 1978 as estrangement, as alienation". This alienated existence also confronts people in a hostile way through state institutions and bureaucracies. The overwhelming majority of the population have no direct control, access to or involvement in the running of the state. Occasionally we are consulted through a general or local election. We have the right to choose our rulers – but not the right to rule. The state's key functions include:

▶ maintaining the degree of social and institutional stability necessary for production, commerce and trade
▶ developing a legal framework that guarantees private property rights and contract law
▶ establishing a universal monetary system
▶ managing external/foreign relations, organising defence and conducting war
▶ maintaining border controls and regulating immigration
▶ regulating the terms and conditions of capital-labour relations
▶ ensuring the supply of new generations of trained and educated workers for the labour market
▶ dealing with the consequences of economic crisis
▶ providing services that capitalists cannot carry out but require such as education, health, transport infrastructure etc
▶ enforcing deductions from people's wages and profits to finance state expenditure.

The state also plays a key ideological role in conveying notions that, for example, capitalism is really all about "individual freedom" and "consumer choice", that the state governs in the "national interest",

---

An intrinsic unity

A state apparatus operates simultaneously as an expression of class *domination*... and as the *execution* of the supreme rule-making, rule-applying, rule-adjudicating, rule-enforcing and rule-defending tasks of society. These two aspects constitute an intrinsic unity: execution of these tasks is class domination and class political domination is the execution of these tasks.

Göran Therborn, *What does the state do when it rules?* Verso 1978 or encouraging prejudices such as that socialism "destroys initiative" while capitalism "promotes enterprise". Established mainstream political parties, the mass media, employers and the education system all lend support to the status quo with a stream of propaganda and assumptions.

At the heart of the state lies a mailed fist – the use of force, compulsion and punishment for those who refuse or decline to acknowledge the decisions of the state. The power of coercion, which in ancient times rested within communities, was long ago appropriated by the state. Payment of income tax or council tax, for example, is a legal obligation backed by the threat of a fine and/or jail. Occupy a property and the owners will assert their "rights" – and the police will turn up to remove the occupiers by physical force if necessary. Have more than six pickets outside a factory and the police will arrest trade unionists for a breach of the law. Engage in solidarity action and the courts will enforce the law that declares this activity illegal. The state will tap your phone and intercept your emails, and infiltrate your organisation if it is considered "subversive" – and you can do little about it except protest.

In times of self-declared national emergency, the state has since the early 1920s had power to dispense with democratic rights altogether and effectively put the country under military rule by decree. States of emergency have been declared on several occasions during major strikes. The New Labour government opted out of the European Convention on Human Rights on the grounds that a state of emergency existed (and continues to exist on a permanent basis) because of the alleged threat of terrorist attacks and the need to suspend civil liberties to deal with it.

In her book *Democracy Against Capitalism*, Ellen Meiksens Wood explains how the capitalist state is unique in its separation or division into economic and political spheres. In previous epochs, the state was a unified expression of economic power. She adds:

> If we are to understand the unique development of capitalism, then, we must understand how property and class relations, as well as the functions of surplus appropriation and distribution, so to speak liberate themselves from – and yet are served by – the coercive institutions that constitute the state, and develop autonomously... At the same time, these developments had as their necessary condition a new and stronger form of centralised public power. The state divested the

appropriating class of direct political powers and duties not immediately concerned with production and appropriation, leaving them with private exploitative powers purified of public, social functions.

The making of the state

There is nothing permanent or fixed about the forms that the state takes. Clearly the 21st century British state bears little comparison with that of medieval or feudal England, although some remnants of the past like the Royal Family, the Privy Council and the House of Lords, endure to this day. In recent decades, the state has altered its form to accommodate the emergence of globalised capitalism at the expense of workers in Britain and other countries (see chapter 4). An overview of the evolution of the British state, through a long and frequently bloody conflict between social classes, shows how it came eventually to assume a capitalist form.

The first decisive political move in the direction of the modern state was the execution of King Charles I in 1649 by Cromwell's revolutionary forces after an historic trial for waging war on his own people. When Charles I was led to out to the scaffold in Whitehall and laid his head on the executioner's block, it marked the definitive end of feudal absolutism and the monarchy's claim to rule as God's divine power in England. The English Revolution – the country was a republic for 11 years – opened the door to a further revolution in ideas, science and the expansion of trade by merchants and investors freed from the tyranny of arbitrary rule. The removal of Charles II by Parliament in 1688 and its invitation to William of Orange to take the throne, reaffirmed and extended this transfer of political power from the court to the Commons. The Act of Settlement of 1701 affirming the independence of the judiciary owed everything to the desire to be free from arbitrary pressures and unilateral decisions imposed by the monarchy.

What character did the new state assume, in the sense of what class interests did it come to reflect? The merchants and landowners/farmers were the new, unchallenged power in the land. America, Ireland, Jamaica and Barbados were already colonial possessions and the English fleet was the most powerful in Europe after defeating the Dutch. After the so-called Glorious Revolution of 1688, the mechanisms were put in place for the rapid expansion of economic activity. In 1694, the Bank of England was created as a lender to the government and the issuer of bank notes. A system of national finance and national debt was created for the first time. With commodity circulation beginning to increase under the emerging capitalist form of production, paper money was vital as a mean of exchange. Institutions evolved for the buying and selling of government stocks, and for providing credit for a variety of government enterprises, mainly overseas.

A bankrupt Scotland was linked with England in 1707 in an Act of Union, which opened the way for Scotland to develop as an industrial country and for its scientists to play a vital role in developing new technologies. The ruling classes' ambitions were facilitated by a more powerful, interventionist state. While ministers nominally remained representatives of the crown in parliament, they began to assert their independence from the monarch. Control of the powerful fleet now rested with the government and not the monarchy. By 1724, Sir Robert Walpole had effectively established himself as Britain's first prime minister and conducted foreign policy directed towards an expansion of trade and colonial possessions. The Seven Years' War, which began in 1756, was the first conflict waged on a global scale, and was fought in Europe, India, North America, the Caribbean, the Philippines and coastal Africa. Britain's victory over France enabled the East India Company to transform itself from a commercial into a military and territorial power. The company took control of Bengal in 1757 and went on to acquire further areas of India and other parts of Asia. Indian policy was until 1773 influenced by shareholders' meetings. This led to state intervention. The Regulating Act (1773) and Pitt's India Act (1784) established government control of political policy through a regulatory board responsible to Parliament.

The beginnings of the agricultural revolution, with new machinery and crops, spurred on the enclosure of common land and the ending of the open field system. Between 1760-1793, there were no fewer than 1,355 Parliamentary Acts which applied to the enclosure of specific estates and parishes. Land was brought together to the advantage of the richer landlords. Smaller holders often had no legal title but depended on custom and tradition. These were routinely ignored by the commissioners appointed to oversee enclosure. Small farmers, who lost their grazing rights, joined the swelling numbers of landless labourers driven into the towns.

As John Saville notes in his book, *The consolidation of the capitalist state 1800-1850*:

> Throughout the 18th century and down to 1832, the landed aristocracy in the House of Lords, and their sons and relatives and the gentry in the Commons, gathered to themselves all the political and administrative offices of government and the country in general. This assembly of power and positions included a massive trawl of government finances for their own benefit and for use in widespread patronage, not least among their own relatives.

During the last quarter of the 18th century, another powerful social force began to appear which would soon challenge this order. The Industrial Revolution, linked closely with inventions in cotton spinning, steam power and iron smelting, accelerated the growth of the capitalist system of production. With it came new classes – the manufacturers and the working class. Each in its own way would contest the power of the state itself.

Agitation for the reform of a corrupt Parliament gathered pace after the end of the war with France in 1815. An alliance of the rising bourgeoisie and workers demanded the vote. They were accompanied by mass assemblies and serious rioting against which the state could do little. By 1832, England seemed on the verge of a revolution against the landed classes. They gave way just in time and extended the franchise – but only to the manufacturers and rising middle class. Workers who had provided the backbone for the movement for reform were abandoned.

Free trade and free markets became the mantra alongside the creation of state forces that would put down disorder and resistance. These were aimed at the new working class, who were fighting for free

Masters and servants

The voice of the manufacturers made itself heard in the Master and Servant Law of 1823. This gave employers remedies for breach of contract over their workers and remained in force until the last quarter of the 19th century. A worker who broke a contract could be summarily sentenced by a local magistrate to jail and hard labour for up to three months - and required to resume his contract after coming out of prison!

trade unions, social justice and, above all, the right to vote and change society (see chapter 2). The first acts of the reformed Parliament were to impose a discipline on trade unions and the workers drawn into the towns by industrialisation. In 1834 six Dorset agricultural workers were convicted of taking an illegal oath when they formed a union branch and were sentenced to transportation. Unions were not to obtain full legal independence until 1875. In the same year as Tolpuddle, the Elizabethan poor law – which provided parish relief to the destitute – was replaced by the hated workhouse in the New Poor Law of 1834. In Saville's view

> In the medium and long term, the New Poor Law of 1834 was perhaps the most important piece of social legislation passed during the 19th century. Its influence was far-reaching, both in daily practice and in the evolution of social consciousness. It confirmed the general belief in self-help which the middle classes preached daily, and over time it entered at least in part into the thinking of working people. Acceptance of parish relief became an article of shame for many sections of the working population – to have a pauper's funeral was an unthinkable disgrace – and in these ways the social stigma and fear of the workhouse went some way towards creating the ethos and ideas which industrial capitalism required of its working force.

The new state set about creating the means to enforce its rule. During the 1830s and 1840s, the first professional police force in the world was established, first in London and then throughout the country. A

Landed interests

The Reform Act [1832] left political power in the hands of the traditional ruling class, the landed interests. They dominated the two Houses of Parliament; they continued to provide the membership of Cabinets of both Whig and Tory governments; they still controlled the patronage of the administration in Whitehall; and the established Church and the armed forces remained untouched. Economic, social and administrative changes were, however, already in train and would lead society to adapt to the political and social requirements of the developing capitalist order.

John Saville, *The consolidation of the capitalist state 1800-1850*. Pluto 1994 professional army was also created with its own barracks in the major industrial towns. Before this, soldiers had been recruited exclusively to fight foreign wars and had been billeted in ordinary people's homes. They were now removed from civilian influence as the state took on a more impersonal and alienated character, removing itself from the population as a whole. The Royal Commission on the Police of 1839 reported that the creation of a force throughout the country would avoid the "painful conflict", of "neighbour versus neighbour" or "master against servant". There was a strong case, it argued, for a "trained and independent force for action in such emergencies" and in this way "the **constitutional authority** of the supreme executive is thus emphatically asserted" [emphasis added]. The police were given distinctive blue uniforms to distinguish them from the military in a bid to make them seem more "independent" along the lines advocated by the Royal Commission.

The development of capitalism also made it possible to levy taxes in a more comprehensive way than before, when excise duty was the only source of state revenue. First introduced in 1799 by William Pitt to finance the war against France, income tax was abolished in 1816 when the conflict ended. The Tories reintroduced income tax in 1842 as a growing budget deficit required a new source of funds and it has remained in being ever since. The 1835 Municipal Corporations Act made over to the wealthier sections of the middle classes the political control of their towns. Before then, the towns had been the private fiefdoms of "freemen", whose number could range from a dozen to 5,000. The unreformed boroughs were generally regarded as a licence to print money and the great majority were dens of corruption, nepotism and indifference to their populations. In 1846, the Corn Laws, which kept domestic prices artificially high, were abolished after a long campaign and confirmed that real power now lay in the hands of the free trade manufacturers and not the landowners. The notion of shareholders and limited liability for directors was introduced in 1856 to help with the raising of capital by industry. A Patent Office was established in 1852 to amend laws unchanged since the early 17th century.

So by the mid-1850s, the unfettered power of the landed aristocracy had been overcome and the new capitalist class had achieved political power. Ordinary working people still did not have the right to vote, despite the best efforts of the Chartists. By 1867 – when the urban working class finally achieved the vote – the capitalist state had been well and truly consolidated.

The scene was set for the rapid expansion of the British colonial empire, which until the 19th century had been formed of self-managing enterprises and acquisitions as a result of wars with France. Wealth accumulated from the slave trade between Africa and the Caribbean colonies accelerated the development of capitalism in Britain. The restless expansion of capital changed the nature of the state, turning it outward in search of raw materials to support domestic production and foreign markets for the resulting commodities. The abolition of the slave trade in 1807 led to new forms of exploitation of human labour and resources through empire. From 1838, the East India Company became a managing agency for the British government in India and lost even this role after the Indian Mutiny of 1857. From then on, India was the jewel in the crown of empire. Until the 1850s, the Colonial Office had been part of the Home Office. Now it had its own department and staff. British control was extended to Fiji, Tonga, Papua, and other islands in the Pacific Ocean, and Britain's acquisition of Burma was completed in 1886. Its conquest of the Punjab and of Balochistan provided substantial new territory in the Indian subcontinent itself.

Elsewhere, British influence in the Far East expanded with the development of the Straits Settlements and the federated Malay states, and in the 1880s protectorates were formed over Brunei and Sarawak. Hong Kong island became British in 1841, and an "informal empire" operated in China by way of British treaty ports and the great trading city of Shanghai. The greatest 19th century extension of British power took place in Africa, however. During the last quarter of the century, Britain took control of Egypt, Sudan, Nigeria, the Gold Coast (now Ghana) and The Gambia. What are now Kenya, Uganda, Zimbabwe, Zambia and Malawi became colonies. Britain sent 500,000 soldiers to the Boer War of 1899-1902 and its costly victory enabled it to create the Union of South Africa in 1910. By the end of the 19th century, the British Empire comprised nearly one-quarter of the world's land surface and more than one-quarter of its total population. These possessions were protected by the mightiest navy in the world and vast armies. A huge bureaucracy co-ordinated the military and civil aspects of empire, ruling over hundreds of millions of people.

2

The struggle for democracy

There are several enduring myths about the present state and democracy. They suggest that capitalism and democracy are natural partners and that the ruling elites have championed the rights of ordinary people since time immemorial. In fact, there is an absolute contradiction in the relationship, which explains why the British parliamentary democratic state is so limiting and limited. It is certainly far removed from the Greek origins of the word – *demos* (people) and *kratos* (rule or power). Exploding these myths will help us reconnect with a people's history of the struggle for democracy in Britain.

Extending power to the people was definitely on the minds of the Levellers, whose demands prompted the first-ever debates in England about a written constitution. The Levellers' movement came to prominence during the civil wars between Parliamentary forces under Oliver Cromwell and Charles I, which lasted from 1641-9. The Levellers had no coherent manifesto or platform but generally shared a belief in popular sovereignty, natural rights, an extended franchise, equality before the law, and religious toleration. They also pioneered the use of petitions and pamphleteering for political ends.

The circumstances of the historic debates, held in St Mary's church next to the Thames at Putney between October and November 1647, were themselves pretty amazing. Charles I was under arrest at nearby Hampton Court while Parliament was under the control of Presbyterians who still wanted to make a deal with the King, despite five years of bloodshed and heavy loss of life. Cromwell had built and led the revolutionary New Model Army, a trained and disciplined force that had routed royalist forces. But Cromwell and his generals were themselves still uncertain what to do with the King. Democracy had established a foothold in the New Model Army. Pamphlets written by men like John "free born" Lilburne circulated freely. They denounced the existing parliament and unrelentingly criticised those who wielded power. They wanted more for the soldiers who had done the fighting against the king. Regiments elected representatives or "agitators" to the Army Council and these were recognised by the commanders.

By September 1647, however, at least five regiments of Cavalry had elected new unofficial agitators and produced a pamphlet called *The Case of the Army Truly Stated*. It was presented to the commander-in-chief, Sir Thomas Fairfax, on 18 October 1647. The soldiers demanded the dissolution of Parliament within a year and substantial changes to the constitution of future parliaments, which were to be regulated by an unalterable "law paramount". With the King under arrest, the Army Council boldly decided to bring the issues into the open and perhaps find a way forward out of the political deadlock they found themselves in. Civilian agitators as well as soldiers were invited to Putney to debate the issues. Cromwell and the "Grandees" of the army, as the generals were dubbed, were in for a big surprise, however. On the morning of 28 October 1647, when proceedings opened, the Levellers dropped a bombshell. *The Case of the Army Truly Stated* – already denounced by Cromwell – was suddenly put to one side in favour of a new, shorter document – *An Agreement of the People*.

The Agreement set out the principles of parliamentary government elected by "the people" that would rule the country, have the power to pass laws and make war. The present Parliament was to be dissolved and a new one elected for a period of two years. As to the power of this Parliament, it would be "inferior only to theirs who choose them" and be limited by "whatsoever is not expressly or impliedly reserved by the represented to themselves".

The Agreement then set out five framework principles:

1. Freedom of conscience – "That matters of religion and the ways of God's worship are not at all entrusted by us to any human power"
2. Freedom from "impresting and constraining any of us to serve in the wars", which is "against our freedom"
3. An amnesty for all those who had said or done anything in the civil war, referred to as "the late public differences"
4. All laws must apply to everyone in the same way, that "no tenure, estate, charter, degree, birth, or place do confer any exemption"
5. Parliament could pass no laws "evidently destructive to the safety and well-being of the people".

The subsequent debate was recorded, although the transcript was lost until 1890. You can almost feel the shock that must have gone round the Army Council once the Grandees had taken in the substance of the Agreement. If they were in any doubt about what was to come, Edward Sexby, agitator and trooper, set the tone. The most powerful advocate of the rights of the common soldier told Cromwell bluntly:

> The cause of our misery is upon two things. We sought to satisfy all men, and it was well; but in going about to do it we have dissatisfied all men. We have laboured to please a king and I think, except we go about to cut all our throats, we shall not please him; and we have gone to support an house which will prove rotten studs – I mean the Parliament, which consists of a company of rotten members.

After *An Agreement of the People* had been read out, Cromwell quickly admitted: "Truly this paper does contain in it very great alterations of the very government of the kingdom, alterations from that government that it hath been under, I believe I may almost say, since it was a nation... Give me leave to say this. There will be very great mountains in the way of this." And that from a man who had already climbed several mountains to build an army to defeat a king. When the debate resumed the next morning, the penny had dropped. Henry Ireton, commissary-general of the army and Cromwell's son-in-law, said if it was intended that "an inhabitant is to be equally considered, and to have an equal voice in the election of those representers, the persons that are for the general Representative", then he was against it. The riposte – which has gone down in history – came not from a Leveller but from Colonel Thomas Rainborough, who told Ireton that his understanding was right, adding:

> For really I think that the poorest he that is in England hath a life to live, as the greatest he; and therefore truly, sir, I think it's clear, that every man that is to live under a government ought first by his own consent to put himself under that government; and I do think that the poorest man in England is not at all bound in a strict sense to that government that he hath not had a voice to put himself under.

Ireton insisted that only those who had property should be able to vote, while Cromwell warned that the consequence "tends to anarchy, must end in anarchy; for where is there any bound or limit set if you take away this limit, that men that have no interest but the interest of breathing shall have no voice in elections?". Rainborough was contemptuous of this argument, and asked what soldiers had fought for: "He hath fought to enslave himself, to give power to men of riches, men of estates, to make him a perpetual slave."

The debate ended in stalemate and the civil war resumed shortly afterwards. Cromwell repressed the Levellers' movement and Charles I was executed in 1649 after a public trial for crimes against his own people. Britain became a republic, which lasted for 11 years.

The Radical movement

But the Levellers' ideas and principles lived on and were taken up again in Britain in the 1760s by John Wilkes. He was a radical journalist and MP who in 1762 launched the *North Briton* to attack the government. One particular attack resulted in the government issuing a general warrant for the arrest of "the authors, printers and publishers" of a "seditious and treasonable paper". Wilkes and 48 others were arrested. Wilkes, as an MP, was sent to the Tower, awaiting trial. But the Lord Chief Justice declared general warrants to be illegal and contrary to the Bill of Rights. Wilkes was expelled from the Commons in 1764 on trumped-up charges and fled to France, returning in 1768 to secure re-election. Wilkes won not once but three times, with the government declaring each election void. Eventually, Wilkes was jailed.

In 1769 the friends and supporters of Wilkes formed the Society for the Supporters of the Bill of Rights (SSBR) to uphold his cause and pay his debts. By 1771 the SSBR called for shorter Parliaments, a wider franchise and the abolition of aristocratic "pocket boroughs". Wilkes decided to report parliamentary debates, to name speakers and comment on events. Attempts to arrest him for this were thwarted and Wilkes became a popular hero. Although he held reactionary views later in life, Wilkes foreshadowed the emergence of the Radical movement for political rights later in the century.

The immediate inspiration of the Radical movement was the French Revolution of 1789 and the American constitution of 1787. Its chief propagandist was Tom Paine, who articulated the novel – for Britain – ideas of democracy. He had cut his teeth in the American Revolution against British rule which ended with a Declaration of Independence in 1776. Paine may have even helped write some of the text. The British ruling class presided over a corrupt state, with an electoral system that viewed the right to vote as a privilege to be bought and sold. Parliament was dominated by great landed proprietors and the electoral map had not been revised since the Middle Ages. Phantom "constituencies" with no inhabitants sent MPs to Westminster – the famous rotten boroughs. London had four MPs while sparsely populated Cornwall had 44. Voting was by a show of hands and a voter might even have to write the candidate's name opposite his own in public!

Soon after the 1789 revolution, France's National Assembly approved a declaration which declared that "ignorance, neglect, or contempt of the rights of man are the sole cause of public calamities and of the corruption of governments". It set forth what it called "a solemn declaration of the natural, unalienable, and sacred rights of man" in 17 articles. They included the statement that:

> Law is the expression of the general will. Every citizen has a right to participate personally, or through his representative, in its foundation. It must be the same for all, whether it protects or punishes. All citizens, being equal in the eyes of the law, are equally eligible to all dignities and to all public positions and occupations, according to their abilities, and without distinction except that of their virtues and talents.

Although the bourgeois revolution stressed the right to property, its profound democratic sides, the targeting of the landed aristocracy and the involvement of the plebeian masses were too much for the reactionaries in London. The idea that all citizens were born and remain "free in equal rights" and that "social distinctions may be founded only upon the general good" had them spluttering into their glasses of port. The Anglo-Irish political philosopher Edmund Burke spoke for them all in his book *Reflections on the French Revolution*, published in 1790. He warned against the potential "crimes of new democracy" and raged against the dangers posed by the intervention of the masses, which he described as "the swinish multitude".

The Radical movement struck back, inspired by Paine. His direct response to Burke was his *Rights of Man*, Part 1 of which was published in 1791. It was a sensation, with the legal sales amounting to nearly 200,000 copies within two years. As for Burke's contention that the British system was set in stone, Paine responded:

> There never did, there never will, and there never can, exist a Parliament, or any description of men, or any generation of men, in any country, possessed of the right or the power of binding and controlling posterity to the "end of time," or of commanding for ever how the world shall be governed, or who shall govern it; and therefore all such clauses, acts or declarations by which the makers of them attempt to do what they have neither the right nor the power to do, nor the power to execute, are in themselves null and void. Every age and generation must be as free to act for itself in all cases as the age and generations which preceded it. The vanity and presumption of governing beyond the grave is the most ridiculous and insolent of all tyrannies.

Paine was for political equality and against privilege and for representative government. He had contempt for hereditary and monarchical principles. His social policy proposals for the abolition of the poor law, a graded estate duty, disarmament, child and maternity benefits, national education and provision of work for the unemployed were far ahead of their time. They influenced radical, egalitarian politics for most of the following century too. Inevitably, the state struck back, prosecuting the book for sedition and forcing Paine to flee the country to France, where he was elected a member of the National Convention.

Reform societies sprang up all over the country. One of the biggest was the London Corresponding Society (LCS). Set up in 1792, it soon had 3,000 members paying a weekly subscription. Its objects were brief – universal suffrage and annual parliaments. Other societies were outright republican in their aims. In Sheffield, the Secretary of War's emissary found in Sheffield 2,500 of the "lowest mechanics" enrolled in a reform society and that the "seditious doctrines of Paine" were in evidence in the town. In November, thousands marched in Sheffield to celebrate the successes of the French army against the crowns of Europe. In May 1792, a Royal Proclamation against seditious publications was issued, aimed at the *Rights of Man*.

The reform movement survived the backlash that followed the start of the war between France and England in early 1793. But the plan to call a National Convention of British reformers, and the forging of links with the United Irishmen movement for a democratic republic sparked a wave of repressions. Scottish reformers who held a Convention were sentenced to transportation to Australia, some dying on the way. Delegates from England to a second Convention in Edinburgh, including key leaders of the Radical movement, were also arrested and transported and died soon after arrival. Despite the setbacks, and the suspension of *Habeas Corpus* by the Pitt government – the suspension lasted for eight years – the reformers called a mass rally in June 1795 at St George's Field in Southwark, the traditional venue for anti-government assemblies and riots. Some sources say 100,000 attended to hear Citizen John Gales Jones tell them:

> Are we Britons, and is not liberty our birthright?... Bring forth your whips and racks, ye ministers of vengeance. Produce your scaffolds... Erect barracks in every street and bastilles in every corner! Persecute and banish every innocent individual; but you will no succeed... The holy blood of patriotism, streaming from the severing axe, shall carry with it the infant seeds of Liberty...

The movement gathered pace as soaring food prices and shortages resulting from the war with France led to hardship and disturbances around the country. There were occasions when the militia took the side of rioters demanding bread. A revolutionary mood swept the country and up to 150,000 rallied in Islington in October, where a

Remonstrance was addressed to the King. It asked: "Wherefore, in the midst of apparent plenty, are we thus compelled to starve? Why, when we incessantly toil and labour, must we pine in misery and want? ... Parliamentary Corruption... like a foaming whirlpool, swallows the fruits of all our labours." Three days later, the anger boiled over when the King was on his way to open Parliament. He was booed and his carriage attacked. "Down with Pitt!" "No War!" "No King!" were among the slogans. The response of the authorities was immediate. A proclamation against seditious assemblies was issued and Pitt brought in the Two Acts, which made it a treasonable offence to incite hatred of the government, constitution or monarch. Magistrates had to be informed of all meetings of more than 50 people.

Another great rally before the legislation came into force marked the end of the popular revolt. Some activists went underground and probably helped inspire the naval mutinies in 1797. Pitt passed more laws, banning the taking of oaths and the Combination Acts of 1799-1800, which illegalised trade unions. This signified that a new social force – the working class – was emerging out of capitalist development. Summing up this period of struggle for rights, the historian E.P. Thomson, in his classic *The Making of the English Working Class*, says:

> It is wrong to see this [period] as the end, for it was also a beginning. In the 1790s, something like an 'English Revolution' took place, of profound importance in shaping the consciousness of the post-war working class... the French Revolution *consolidated* Old Corruption in uniting landowners and manufacturers in a common panic; and the popular societies were too weak and too inexperienced to effect either revolution or reform on their own.

The new working class made itself felt at the end of the war with France. In 1819, up to 80,000 workers gathered with their banners at St Peter's Field, Manchester, to demand parliamentary reform. Local magistrates summoned the military to arrest the leaders and disperse the crowd. They killed 15 and wounded hundreds more in what became known as the Peterloo Massacre.

The Chartists

By 1838, when the great Chartist movement was launched against the state, Britain had been radically transformed – politically, economically and socially. These new conditions account for the revolutionary, insurrectionary character of Chartism over a 20-year period. The rising manufacturing class, following the Reform Act of 1832, was now sharing power with the landed aristocracy in Parliament and soon after wrested control of the major towns. Under the threat of revolution by the masses, the old elite had caved in. The workers were left without the vote, abandoned by their middle-class "allies". Within a few decades, capitalist production had firmly rooted itself throughout the land. Factories sprang up in towns and valleys as the industrial revolution marched on. Men, women and children worked in the most appalling conditions, living in the foulest housing and dire poverty. These were the years of wholesale enclosure, when common grazing rights were lost in villages and landless labourers forced to move to the towns. Domestic industries were destroyed by rampant capitalism amid this catastrophe for ordinary people.

By the mid-1830s, however, the working class had established its identity and its conflict of interest with the employers. Trade unions, friendly societies, periodicals and even the rudiments of political parties gave organisational form to this consciousness. The demand for political power soon followed. The Chartists were the first working class mass movement anywhere in the world. Their Six Points published in 1838 were for annual parliaments, universal manhood suffrage, payment of MPs, secret ballot, equal electoral districts and abolition of property qualifications for MPs. The enactment of the Six Points would undoubtedly have meant the overthrow of the industrialists and the aristocracy.

Having separated themselves from the middle-class reformers and free trade campaigners, the Chartists involved millions of people in petitions, strikes, meetings, conventions, national organisation and insurrections in a direct challenge to the state.

The first major rally took place in Glasgow when tens of thousands reportedly marched. But in September 1838 the authorities were shocked when an estimated 300,000 assembled at Kersal Moor near Manchester as manufacturers closed their factories for the day. "For Children and Wife we'll War to the Knife", and "Bread and Revolution" were typical slogans carried by Chartists. A similar sized rally took place at Peep Green, between Leeds and Huddersfield.

Early in 1839, the Convention of the Industrious Classes met in London before moving to Birmingham in May. Delegates had been elected by mass meetings in the months before and many workers considered the Convention an expression of the coming government of workers – an alternative to the existing state. The Convention had to decide what to do in the event that Parliament rejected the petition. Delegates adopted the formula of "peaceably if we may, forcibly if we must". A manifesto of "ulterior measures" included a month's general strike, a resort to arms and a trade boycott. The government despatched 6,000 troops to northern England and banned armed assemblies. Then in May Parliament duly threw the petition out, even though it had had 1,200,000 signatures – a massive number considering the population as a whole was only about 16 million. The debate between the advocates of moral force as opposed to physical force within Chartism became academic as the anger of supporters grew. Uprisings were prepared throughout the country but the only serious attempt to carry one out was in Newport, South Wales, where it was defeated by the military. A strike call proved unsuccessful. Many Chartists were arrested. The *Northern Star*, the voice of the Chartists edited by Feargus O'Connor, had a circulation of 35,000 copies a week in 1839. It kept Chartists all over the country informed about each other's activities and presented news from a working-class point of view.

The next phase of the movement began in 1840 with the founding of the National Charter Association, generally regarded as the first organised party of labour in the world. The petition of 1842 attracted an amazing 3,317,702 signatures. Its list of grievances went beyond the Six Points to include the Poor Law, restrictions on the right of public meetings, the new police force and the conditions of workers in town and countryside. One of their leaders, George Harney, declared that in the event of the dissolution of parliament before the Charter could be presented, the people should "take their affairs into their own hands... let the people of each county, city and borough, wherever democracy hath reared its head" set about electing delegates "furnished with a bodyguard of sturdy sans culottes" organised "according to the strength of the democracy in the district". "What army", he asked, "could resist a million of armed men? ... Within a week not a despot's breath would pollute the air of England."

In 1842, a massive strike wave – the first in the capitalist world – broke out in northern England and western Scotland after MPs once more rejected the petition. The strike was spurred on by a general fall in wages. The "general strike" involved up to 500,000 workers at its peak. The strike began with the encouragement of some manufacturers, who shut their factories. Their aim was to use the power of the Chartists to force the Tory government to repeal the Corn Laws and move faster towards free trade. But this move backfired, as neither the Chartists nor the workers were supporters of free trade. What motivated them more was the struggle for the 10-hour day and the repeal of the Poor Laws.

Before long, the employers joined in the attacks on the strikers. Some Chartists hoped that a revolution might be built from this movement. But the capitalist state, at first taken aback by the developments, now deployed its new-found powers. Troops broke up meetings, killing four at Preston and the strike collapsed after an heroic two months of struggle. Post-strike repression was widespread, with up to 1,500 brought before the lower courts and special commissions. Some 200 were transported, some for life, while key leaders were jailed.

In 1848, galvanised by the revolution in France, the Chartist movement made a final attempt to win its demands through a petition backed by a demonstration of over 200,000 at Kennington, across the river from Westminster. The government feared that the April 10 rally would signal the start of a revolution and Queen Victoria was moved out of London. Troops and police blocked the bridges across the Thames. Once more the petition was rejected. The Chartists then convened a National Assembly for May 1 as a would-be rival seat of power to Parliament. Its aim was to continue sitting until the Charter was law. The Assembly set out a policy agenda that went far beyond the Charter. It voted to repeal the union between Britain and Ireland; it backed a call to sever the connection between church and state; it carried a motion advocating the employment of the poor on public lands and another that recommended the people to arm. But plans for an insurrection in August were easily thwarted by the forces of the state and the high point of Chartism passed.

While the Chartists did not succeed in their immediate aims, their effect on the workers' movement was lasting and profound. Frederick Engels, who inherited a factory in Manchester, got to know the Chartist leaders in the area and he wrote in *The condition of the working class in England*, 1845:

> Since the working-men do not respect the law, but simply submit to its power when they cannot change it, it is most natural that they should at least propose alterations in it, that they should wish to put a proletarian law in the place of the legal fabric of the bourgeoisie. This proposed law is the People's Charter, which in form is purely political, and demands a democratic basis for the House of Commons. Chartism is the compact form of their opposition to the bourgeoisie.

He explained how the Chartists movement had helped to form class solidarity, identity and consciousness. This became clear during the bourgeoisie's agitation for the repeal of the Corn Laws in the interests of free trade. Engels noted:

> Free competition has caused the workers suffering enough to be hated by them; its apostles, the bourgeoisie, are their declared enemies. The working-man has only disadvantages to await from the complete freedom of competition. The demands hitherto made by him, the Ten Hours' Bill, protection of the workers against the capitalist, good wages, a guaranteed position, repeal of the New Poor Law, all of the

Political accommodation

The effective consolidation of the British state by the third quarter of the 19th century was a product of a rapidly developing industrial society, of a middle class whose ideology of laissez-faire and the free market was a central article of faith linked with an unshakeable belief in a confident future. The political reforms of the 1830s and 1840s brought the traditional ruling class and owners of capital into a political accommodation which above all recognised the need for unity against the threats to the rights of property. A turbulent and dissatisfied working people was not helpful, and although their activities could be contained by oppressive laws and improved policing, it was their political attitudes that finally had to be confronted, and defeated. That was the meaning of 1848, and for the rich and powerful, and their middle-class allies, it was a famous victory.

John Saville, *The consolidation of the capitalist state 1800-1850*. Pluto 1994 things which belong to Chartism quite as essentially as the "Six Points," are directly opposed to free competition and Free Trade.

While for the capitalist class the six points of the Charter were the "beginning and end of the matter", for workers they were a means to further ends. "Political power our means, social happiness our end," is now the clearly formulated war-cry of the Chartists, said Engels. After 1843, he worked closely with the Chartist leader George Harney and introduced into the working class movement the ideas of revolutionary communism which he and Karl Marx were developing.

The right to vote

This brief survey of three powerful movements for democracy demonstrates that the formation of a state designed to protect private property and the rights of capital, was bitterly contested by the masses who were excluded from exercising power altogether. Men in towns finally got the vote in 1867, while those in rural areas had to wait until 1884. As for women, they had to sacrifice themselves in often violent struggle in the Suffragette movement before first achieving a limited franchise in 1918.

What was conceded in the 19th century was limited to a representative democracy – the sending of MPs to Parliament to represent the interests of their constituents. The concept of representative democracy had been developed in America by James Madison in the period following the declaration of independence from Britain in 1776. Until then,

---

A late arrival

Democracy, whether parliamentary or otherwise, was thus a latecomer on the British political scene. It was a novel feature grafted on to a pre-existing constitutional structure. Largely for that reason, democracy in Britain, in the form of universal suffrage, was accepted as a humdrum matter of political practice long before any widespread enthusiasm developed for democracy as a set of political ideals that deserved to be promoted for its own sake.

Anthony King, The British Constitution. CUP 2007

The Suffragettes

In 1897, various local and national suffrage organisations came together under the banner of the National Union of Women's Suffrage Societies (NUWSS) specifically to campaign for the vote for women. The NUWSS was constitutional in its approach, preferring to lobby parliament with petitions and hold public meetings. The Women's Social and Political Union (WSPU) was founded as a breakaway movement at the Pankhurst family home in Manchester on 10 October 1903 by six women, including Emmeline and Christabel Pankhurst, who soon emerged as the group's leaders. To illustrate their more militant stance, they adopted the slogan "Deeds, not words". Around the turn of the century, a subgroup called the Women's Tax Resistance League, using the slogan "No Vote, No Tax," began a campaign of tax resistance.

In 1906, the WSPU began a series of actions. Members chained themselves to railings, set fire to public and private property and disrupted speeches both at public meetings and in the House of Commons. Members of the WSPU and other militant groups such as the Women's Freedom League were known as "suffragettes". In 1908 the WSPU adopted purple, white and green as its official colours, and held a 300,000-strong rally in Hyde Park. They also opened a chain of shops to raise money. Many suffragettes went to prison as a result of their actions and often chose to go on hunger strike in support of their cause and to demand political prisoner status. Some were force fed against their will. The government later passed what was commonly referred to as the Cat and Mouse Act, which allowed the release of suffragettes when near to death due to lack of food, but they could be re-imprisoned once fit again.

the only existing historical experience of democracy in action was in ancient Greece in the 4th Century BCE. Aristotle's classic definition of democracy was a constitution in which "the free-born and poor control the government – being at the same time a majority" as opposed to oligarchy , in which "the rich and better-born control the government – being at the same time a minority".

Athenian democracy was direct and conferred a unique status on subordinate classes. All those entitled to participate (women and slaves were excluded) were also empowered to take decisions. Every Athenian citizen had the right to attend meetings of the Assembly, a meeting of the citizen body which was called more than 40 times per year. Decisions at the Assembly were taken on the basis of a majority vote and any

A new suffrage bill was introduced in 1910, but growing impatient, the WSPU launched a campaign of protest in 1912 on the basis of targeting property and avoiding violence against any person. Initially this involved smashing shop windows, but ultimately escalated to burning stately homes and bombing public buildings including Westminster Abbey. In 1913 Emily Davison threw herself in front of the King's horse at the Epsom Derby and later died of her injuries.

Included in the many militant acts performed were the burning of churches, restaurants and railway carriages, smashing government windows weekly, cutting telephone lines, spitting at police and politicians, partial destruction of the then Chancellor of the Exchequer David Lloyd George's home, cutting and burning pro-suffrage slogans into stadium turf, sending letter bombs, destroying greenhouses at Kew Gardens, chaining themselves to railings and blowing up houses.

The East London Federation of mostly working class women and led by Sylvia Pankhurst was expelled in 1914. She rejected the WPSU's support for the First World War. The group evolved into the Workers' Socialist Federation and for a brief period Pankhurst was a member of the newly founded Communist Party of Great Britain and attended meetings in Moscow organised by the Bolsheviks. As a result of campaigns dating back to the mid-nineteenth century, some women over 30 were finally granted the vote in 1918. However, this right was not achieved for all women until the end of the 1920s.

proposals which were passed by a majority became law. Because every citizen had the right to speak and to vote at the Assembly, every citizen had the chance of directly determining what the laws should be.

James Madison, one of the key architects of the American constitution, was, however, concerned with how to solve the perceived problem of "majority tyranny". One advantage of the system of representation, he wrote in the *Federalist Papers*, is that it provides a mechanism:

> to refine and enlarge the public views, by passing them through the medium of a chosen body of citizens, whose wisdom may best discern the true interest of their country, and whose patriotism and love of justice will be least likely to sacrifice it to temporary or partial

considerations. Under such a regulation, it may well happen that the public voice, pronounced by the representatives of the people, will be more consonant to the public good than if pronounced by the people themselves, convened for the purpose.

So Madison's objective was clear – to avoid decisions "pronounced by the people themselves". Instead, they would be "represented". Thus the rule of the *demos* was replaced by ideas of limited government. Needless to say, neither slaves nor women were represented in America at this time. Representation was established as a kind of a filter, to deny ordinary people access to power. In *Democracy against capitalism*, Ellen Meiskens Wood insists that representative democracy is not "the *exercise* of political power but its *relinquishment*, its *transfer* to others, its *alienation*".

Debarred from participation

In capitalist society, providing it develops under the most favourable conditions, we have a more or less complete democracy in the democratic republic. But this democracy is always hemmed in by the narrow limits set by capitalist exploitation, and consequently always remains, in effect, a democracy for the minority, only for the propertied classes, only for the rich. Freedom in capitalist society always remains about the same as it was in the ancient Greek republics: freedom for the slave-owners. Owing to the conditions of capitalist exploitation, the modern wage slaves are so crushed by want and poverty that "they cannot be bothered with democracy", "cannot be bothered with politics"; in the ordinary, peaceful course of events, the majority of the population is debarred from participation in public and political life.

V.I. Lenin, *The State and Revolution*. Moscow 1917

At the same time, changes in the nature of the political system weakened the representative system. By the last quarter of the 19th century, power in Britain had already passed from Parliament to the executive in the shape of a prime minister and the government. As a result, Parliament in the shape of the Commons has had little or no effective control or real power for at least 125 years. The constitutional position of the House of Commons is to provide the raw material in the form of MPs who then go off and become something else – the

Trade union rights come and go

Because the state ultimately reflects the requirements of capitalism, rights apparently secured in one period may be taken away in another through fresh legislation. In other words, these rights are relative under capitalism and each generation has to struggle for them.

Take the case of trade union rights. Unions or "combinations" were made illegal in 1799 and although the laws were repealed after the Napoleonic Wars, unions continued to be repressed and attacked by the state throughout the first half of the 19th century. Full legal rights were only won in 1875. They lasted barely 25 years before courts intervened to undermine the right to strike. Union rights were restored after 1906 by the Liberal government, severely curtailed during both world wars, and were effective between 1945 and 1979. Then in the early 1980s the Thatcher governments abolished full rights to strike, picket and take sympathy action. That remains the position today after more than a decade of New Labour rule.

government. The conventional idea that Parliament has lost power only in recent times is also rejected by Anthony King, the political scientist, in his book *The British Constitution*:

> Commentators frequently refer to the decline of parliament – that is, the House of Commons – in recent decades, but parliament's decline as a legislative assembly began in the middle of the 19th century and was complete by, at the latest, the 1880s or 1890s. Nothing much of constitutional significance has happened [to parliament] since then... It goes without saying that the British House of Commons is now, and has been for a very long time, the archetypal arena assembly. It is simply not equipped to function as a transformative legislature, and of course governments of all political parties are anxious to ensure that it never, ever becomes so equipped.

Nevertheless, securing representative democracy was a major historical gain for the working class. It gave them a taste of political power, even if they were kept away from its main levers. Frustrated by attacks of the ruling class parties, the trade unions and socialists were able to establish the Labour Party in 1900 on the understanding that it might one day become the government and be in a position to carry through reforms and policies that could benefit workers. Labour from the outset was a party wedded to the existing state and the parliamentary system and believed that socialism would occur at some distant point as the result of the accumulation of reforms. Despite its gradualist outlook, some sections of the ruling class feared that allowing a Labour government to take office would open the floodgates to revolution. They need not have panicked. The first minority Labour government of 1924 lasted under a year and the 1929 government collapsed in 1931, leading to national government with the Tories under Ramsay MacDonald, who had been Labour prime minister.

In 1945, the soldiers and workers who had played the decisive role in defeating Nazi Germany were determined not to return to the conditions of the 1930s of mass unemployment, poverty and wretched housing conditions. The ousting of war leader Churchill and the landslide victory of the Labour Party with a majority of 145 was a profound shock to the ruling class. Labour's success was in the context of a revolutionary upsurge around Europe alongside the significant role played by the Red Army in crushing Hitler's armies. While Labour set about restoring battered British capitalism on the basis of American loans, the government was driven by popular sentiment to create the welfare state, a mass housing programme and to set up the National Health Service in the teeth of establishment opposition. A huge programme of nationalisation included the railways and the mines. Even after Labour was replaced by the Tories in 1951, most of these reforms remained intact for the next 25 years.

3

A market state

So long as the state could present a democratic façade, and allow reformist parties to make changes that improved the conditions of working people, it has generally retained popular support. In the immediate post-1945 period, the state took on the role as mediator between the classes, softening the harshest of conditions and reining in the excesses of capital. Now the tendency is towards abandoning bourgeois democracy in all the major capitalist states. A new period of corporate-driven globalisation also marks the end of the era when major reforms could be extracted from capitalism.

In Britain, the changes to the state began under the Tories during the Thatcher/Major governments of 1979-1997. In 1984, the Thatcher regime deployed state forces on behalf of the publicly-owned National Coal Board and its plan to close pits. For 12 solid months, massed ranks of police were used to physically confront and attack striking miners, arresting hundreds of pickets and injuring many more. The union's assets were seized as the Tory government made the struggle for jobs a defence of state political power. Behind the scenes, MI5, the internal spy agency, infiltrated the miners' union and staged provocations.

The 1984-5 strike marked the early period of corporate-driven globalisation, which has changed the way capitalism operates. State power is now more openly revealed as the political and ugly face of capitalism, both domestic but particularly transnational. The hard-won rights to representation now count for little. Despite the widespread assumption that capitalist democracy was once the only future worth talking about, the British state no longer has that allure. Popular support is ebbing away as what was once a representative democracy is transformed into a ruthless market state. The state promotes naked commercialism and markets in every sphere of public and civic life. Civil liberties and basic rights are replaced by authoritarianism as the coercive side of the state takes centre stage.

These profound changes coincide with and are ultimately driven by the corporate-led globalisation of the world economy and financial system over the last 35 years. This process has integrated every country into a new global production and financial system. At the heart of the globalisation process are the transnational corporations (TNCs), with their compulsive and restless quest to drive down production costs and expand markets. No more than 100 TNCs, many more powerful than states, working through local partner enterprises, dominate the global economy.

The other key component of the globalised economy are the 24-hour, electronically-controlled financial markets. National borders are a matter of indifference to TNCs and financial markets. Capital transcends borders in search of maximum profit.

Globalisation is, of course, not a new phenomenon but while it pre-dates capitalism, it accelerated rapidly in the 19th century, as Marx and Engels noted in 1848 in their *Communist Manifesto*:

> The bourgeoisie cannot exist without constantly revolutionising the instruments of production, and thereby the relations of production, and with them the whole relations of society... Constant revolutionising of production, uninterrupted disturbance of all social conditions, everlasting uncertainty and agitation distinguish the bourgeois epoch from all earlier ones. All fixed, fast frozen relations, with their train of ancient and venerable prejudices and opinions, are swept away, all new-formed ones become antiquated before they can ossify. All that is solid melts into air, all that is holy is profaned... The need of a

constantly expanding market for its products chases the bourgeoisie over the entire surface of the globe. It must nestle everywhere, settle everywhere, establish connections everywhere.

By the beginning of the 20th century, in a new imperialist epoch, the relentless global expansion of capital led to tensions that could not be contained or controlled within the capitalist nation-state system that had evolved. In August 1914, the British and German states met on the battlefield for control of the world's resources. The British state used the industrial techniques developed by capitalist enterprises to produce an unending supply of arms for the slaughter, which by war's end in 1918 had taken the lives of 20 million people.

Within 20 years, the unresolved contradictions between the state, the nation-state and capitalist economy exploded once again in World War II. The destruction of people, property and productive capacity was on a far greater scale. This time, alongside attempts to re-establish international relations in the United Nations, came recognition of the increasingly dominant global character of finance capital. The International Bank for Reconstruction and Development (IBRD) which became the World Bank and the International Monetary Fund (IMF) were established as part of the 1944 arrangements for managing the world economy.

Globalisation

The contemporary period of globalisation began over 30 years ago in the wake of the break-down of the post-World War II monetary agreements known as Bretton Woods. These were based on fixed exchange rates, tight restrictions on capital flows and trade tariffs organised by an inter-state system. The arrangements which collapsed in on themselves from the late 1960s onwards, were accompanied in the 1970s by economic crisis, inflation and acute class confrontations in all the major capitalist countries. By the early 1980s, capital found support in politicians like Reagan and Thatcher in their quest to "liberate" markets, deregulate financial controls, privatise state industries and introduce "flexible" labour markets. In adapting to the new globalisation process, the state has, however, undermined its own legitimacy, authority and capacity to act with some degree of relative autonomy.

For the state, globalisation is a contradictory and potentially fatal outcome, in the following ways:

▶ the state's role as mediator between class interests has been abandoned in favour of facilitating corporate and financial interests
▶ the state has created markets in public services where none existed before and sold off state-owned enterprises
▶ the state's capacity to influence economic and financial policies has

The World Trade Organisation

Established in 1995, the WTO:

▶ is a permanent institution based in Geneva with a 500-strong secretariat
▶ is the only international body whose authority the United States accepts
▶ opens markets for the benefit of transnational corporations
▶ administers dozens of international trade agreements and declarations
▶ handles and adjudicates on trade disputes
▶ monitors national trade policies
▶ has a legal personality and the power to enforce its rulings
▶ makes rulings which take precedence over agreements such as the Universal Declaration of Human Rights.

The WTO controls:

▶ the General Agreement on Trade in Services, which deregulates public services
▶ Trade Related Intellectual Property Rights, which set enforceable global rules on patents, copyrights, and trademarks
▶ Trade Related Investment Measures, which dictate what governments can and cannot do in regulating foreign investment
▶ Agreement on the Application of Sanitary and Phytosanitary Standards, covering food safety, animal and plant health
▶ Financial Services Agreement, established to remove obstacles to the free movement of financial services corporations
▶ Agreement on Agriculture, setting rules on the international food trade
▶ Agreement on Subsidies and Countervailing Measures, which sets limits on what governments may and may not subsidise
▶ Agreement on Technical Barriers to Trade, set up to limit national regulations that interfere with trade.

narrowed appreciably under globalisation

▶ the democratic mask is increasingly revealed as just that – a political façade with no substance, leading to deep scepticism among voters

▶ nominally neutral bodies like the civil service and intelligence agencies have been politicised and now serve governments' immediate agendas

▶ more and more, "arms-length" state agencies are created which are totally unaccountable at central and local level

▶ local government has been reduced to carrying out government orders and decisions

▶ hard-won social rights and civil liberties are either seriously eroded or abolished altogether

▶ governments are forced to sidestep the rule of law and the independence of the judiciary

▶ mainstream political parties have moved closer to each other in their endorsement of corporate and financial set-ups.

The state at national level increasingly exists only in relation to an emerging transnational state. At the centre of the transnational state are the World Trade Organisation, the International Monetary Fund and the European Union. World trade and investment rules and regulations are determined by the WTO, an unelected, unaccountable body, while the regional framework is set by the EU, another bureaucratic, remote body whose commissioners are appointed.

New role of the state

▶ advancing interests of home-based TNCs
▶ creating conditions favourable for inward FDI
▶ technological intelligence gathering
▶ creating independent technology capacities
▶ promoting innovative capacities, technical competence and technical transfer
▶ creating institutions and structures that support an entrepreneurial climate
▶ promoting supranational national and regional innovation systems
▶ abandoning declining sectors
▶ promoting "sunrise" sectors.

Bob Jessop, *The future of the capitalist state*. 2002

According to political scientist Anthony King, no single development in recent times has done more to alter Britain's basic constitutional structure than membership of the EU. It is difficult to contest his view that "the legal and constitutional consequences of Britain's accession to the Treaty of Rome have been immense". The most significant of these concerns the primacy of European Community law over UK law. As King puts it, "when the two conflict, the former trumps the latter". Furthermore, British courts have had no option but to enforce Community law in Britain. In effect, the Community constitutes a new legal order of international law to which the British state is subordinate. In addition, British citizens were given the right to pursue actions against their own government in European courts. As King explains:

> Under the European Communities Act 1972, the British courts now owe a legal duty to give effect to laws created by a significant power outside the British state. In particular, the British courts now have both a duty and an ability, which they had never before possessed, to refuse to give effect to legislation passed by the British parliament on the grounds that the law in question is in breach of European law ... For all practical purposes and at least for the foreseeable future, the British parliament is no longer sovereign. It has conceded much of its power to the institutions of the European Union and, in so doing, has conceded substantial powers to the British courts.

As the remit and power of the EU has been extended, so too has the power that the EU's institutions can exercise over national governments. The capacity of national governments to veto decisions in the Council of Ministers has been reduced drastically. As King points out, a range of policy fields that were once considered "domestic" now fall wholly or partly within the EU's power:

> Britain could not, even if it wanted to, impose an external tariff on goods imported from any of the other twenty-six EU member states, nor could it, even if it wanted to, impose a tariff other than the common EU tariff on goods coming from outside the EU. But the creation of a functioning single market has also meant in practice the dismantling of quotas and other non-tariff barriers to trade, requiring national governments to put out to competitive tender across Europe the great

majority of public-sector purchases and projects... "

William I. Robinson, in his paper *Global Capitalism and the Transnational State*, insists that this does not mean that the national state has become irrelevant but:

> Rather, the national state is being transformed and increasingly absorbed functionally into a larger transnational institutional structure that involves complex new relations between national states and supra or transnational institutions, on the one hand, and diverse class and social forces, on the other. As national states are captured by transnational capitalist forces they tend to serve the interests of global over local accumulation processes. The TNS [transnational state], for instance, has played a key role in imposing the neo-liberal model on the old Third World and therefore in reinforcing the class relations of global capitalism. (*Societies Without Borders (2)* 2007)

'Hollowing out'

The movement towards an overarching transnational state that subordinates national states in the globalisation process has even alarmed senior capitalist politicians. Some like former US vice-president Al Gore have referred to this process as the "hollowing out" of the state, whereby its former functions are dispersed, diluted or simply transferred to other supra-national bodies. This irresistible process verifies in its own way that state institutions cannot exist independently of the prevailing economic system. While the impact of globalisation on states varies from country to country, Britain is the most enthusiastic champion of an essentially sinister merging of economics and politics.

Far from resisting pressures to adapt and change, New Labour came to power intent on using the state to obliterate as far as possible the boundaries between public and private, between state and corporate power. It has reached the point where citizens and voters are now customers and consumers first and foremost.

What the previous Tory governments from 1979-97 began, New Labour has deepened in a far more systematic way. The Tories, driven by the new, globalised economic conditions, privatised most of the nationalised industries and utilities and shut down others, like coal.

Much of the civil service was decentralised into executive agencies. An internal market was imposed on the National Health Service and local government was compelled to contract out many services. The Tories had moved Britain from a welfare state to what was dubbed a "regulatory state", where the task was to ensure that markets worked properly.

Successive Blair/Brown governments have extended this agenda and turned their administrations into executive management teams of Britain PLC. In doing so, they have transformed their own party into an extension of capitalist rule, abandoning Labour's reformist origins and creating New Labour as an openly pro-business party. Businessmen sit in the government while the trade unions – while continuing to fund New Labour – are left out in the cold, failing to get Tory anti-union laws repealed or persuade the government to protect manufacturing jobs from being exported to China and other cheaper regions of the global economy.

The state has abandoned primary responsibility in a number of areas including pensions (where people are encouraged to take out risky occupational and private pensions), higher education (where students have to take out loans and pay fees) and care in older age (where the private sector is now dominant). Markets have been created in childcare and legal aid provision, in the detention of refugees as well as in the education system where parents have "choice" between different options and types of schools. An astonishing one third of all public services – far more than previously thought – are now in the hands of the private and voluntary sectors, according to a report commissioned by the government and published in July 2008. The research shows that the "public service industry", as it is now called in government and financial circles, has

Business the only business

The truly fundamental change that capitalist globalisation has introduced... is that, for the first time in human history, there is indeed a material and ideological shift towards selling business as such as the only real business of the planet and its inhabitants. So, in the global capitalist system, agents and agencies of the state (among other institutions) fulfil the role of facilitators of the global capitalist project.

Leslie Sklair, *The Transnational Capitalist Class*. 2000

doubled in value in little more than a decade under New Labour, rising from £42 billion in 1995-6 to nearly £80 billion in 2007-8.

The report says that the UK is "a global leader in opening up public service markets to competition". Britain spends a larger share of its gross domestic product in this sector than any other major economy, the report notes proudly. The sector covers everything from health to waste management, IT, "welfare-to-work", training, construction and legal services. The report was commissioned by the Department for Business Enterprise and Regulatory Reform, whose mission is, according to minister John Hutton, "to work to ensure business success in an increasingly competitive world". Hutton led a trade mission to the US to help companies such as Serco, BT and Capita, as well as voluntary providers such as the Shaw Trust, "sell their skills" in running public services. Needless to say, the report was written by a senior figure in the global business world, DeAnne Julius – herself a former director of Serco!

There are no limits to the privatisation of the state and services. On 9 July 2008, James Purnell, work and pensions secretary, told MPs there was now "no ideology about the means" by which welfare-to-work programmes were delivered. Having opened the whole of his department's work up to offers from the voluntary and private sector, he said that if they "can do it more effectively, we should look at that".

By far the largest sector within the "public services industry" is health, accounting for £24 billion of spending last year. The creeping privatisation of the NHS is to speed up under the plans for polyclinics. Richard Branson's Virgin Group is said to be in the frame for running a group of polyclinics in Camden, north London.

Local government has been reduced to what Anthony King calls a "pale shadow of its former self" by both Tories and New Labour. From being able to raise their own revenue locally to spend on services as they saw fit, local authorities are now a mere cipher for central government control. As King explains in *The British Constitution*:

> The story of British local government during the past half-century is in large part a story of its cumulative loss of autonomy, its cumulative loss of freedom and its cumulative loss of power. These losses have been on such a scale that in the early twenty-first century the word "government" in the phrase local government really does need to be put in inverted commas.

Brown's City love-in

On the eve of the credit crunch in summer 2007, and just before he became prime minister, Gordon Brown as chancellor told financiers at the Mansion House how for ten years "the City of London has risen by your efforts, ingenuity and creativity to become a new world leader". Over 40% of the world's foreign equities were traded in London, more than New York, along with over 30% of the world's currency exchanges.

He added: "In a study... of the top 50 financial cities, the City of London came first. So I congratulate you Lord Mayor and the City of London on these remarkable achievements, an era that history will record as the beginning of a new golden age for the City of London". By their efforts, he said, Britain was already second to none "for our openness, pro Europe, pro free trade" and had to maintain "our competitiveness".

That is why the government had cut the main rate of corporation tax to just 28% - the lowest of any of the major economies. In 1982, the rate was 52%.

The details are well established and the changes began when Thatcher's free-market capitalism came up against what King calls the tendency towards "unthinking collectivism" that pervaded local government. Over the following 20 years, the power to raise revenue locally was abolished, local authorities that opposed Tory policies like the Greater London Council were abolished, many services were compulsorily privatised and government started to lay down what could be spent and on what services. Whitehall achieved this through a financial takeover. In the early 1980s, locally-generated revenues amounted to about half of the total; it fell to 15% at the end of the century and is currently around 20%. The government specifies each and every local authority's grant in minute detail.

Deprived of funds to renovate estates, local councils have resorted to transferring vast swathes of their housing stock. The creation of so-called Academy schools by New Labour – which are run independently of councils, alongside the private funding of new schools – has hastened the effective demise of local government. This counter-revolution leads King to conclude that local government is "no longer, in any meaningful sense, a part of the British constitution", having been "imprisoned and disembowelled". In 2008, the research organisation Democratic Audit's review of power and participation in Britain concluded that none of the major parties now questions the pre-eminence of the City

---

State bail-outs

In many cases, when capital moves into a previously non-market sphere, risk is underwritten by the state. When Railtrack failed, the state set up Network Rail to keep the trains running. British Energy, the privatised nuclear power generator, supplying 20% of Britain's electricity, had to be bailed out by the government to the tune of £410m in 2002 to meet the company's debts. Three large long-term local government contracts for corporate services with a £685m value have failed since 2005, leaving the state to pick up the pieces. The failure of Metronet, one of the companies upgrading the part-privatised London Underground network forced the Greater London Authority to step in and offer financial guarantees. The biggest bail-out of them all in the UK was Northern Rock, when £25 billion was pumped into the failing bank. Liberal Democrat spokesman Vince Cable noted that the state had nationalised the risk and privatised the profit.

---

of London and the financial services industry and added:

> In 1997, Labour's leaders finally renounced all intentions of challenging finance and corporate business interests when they reinvented the party as "New Labour".

A "quango" is the colloquial name for a "quasi-autonomous non-governmental organisation". Collectively they encompass many roles and perform many functions in all areas and on behalf of government. In 2006 there were 524 quangos in addition to 272 executive agencies. The NHS is run as a quango while agencies include the Child Support Agency, Highways Agency, the Prison Service, Land Registry and the Identity and Passport Service. The structures of what Democratic Audit calls "quasi-government, or modern governance", rely on business people to fill posts. It's report adds:

> Advisory quangos, or committees, are a low-visibility and low-cost layer of government that shapes decisions on drugs and medicines, the dangers from radioactive waste, hazardous substances, the chemical ingredients of processed foods and drink and other risks, the quality of air people breathe and numerous other sensitive matters that have an immediate bearing on the daily lives of ordinary people. Yet these specialist committees are often filled with members who are direct

representatives of the **relevant businesses** and experts who have personal and professional interests in the **companies and industries** on whose products or plans they sit in judgment. [emphasis added]

What New Labour has done is to remould the state, moving it on from a regulation state to what is effectively a market state. A massive transfer of wealth has taken place, from the public to private sectors, from taxpayers to corporate shareholders. The political effect, of course, has been to remove these state and public service activities even further away from any semblance of democratic accountability, let alone control.

Private clinics doing operations for the NHS are accountable to shareholders. Academies set up to replace "failing schools" are outside of local authority control, allowing them to reject theories of evolution in favour of "intelligent design". The private firms running detention centres are almost certainly part of a global corporation. Your energy supplier may be a French-based transnational and your rail provider is just another company. As Steven Lukes writes in *Worlds of Capitalism* (2005):

> For as privatisation and the contracting out of services has proceeded, the essential link between elector and representative (national or local) is severed. Marketisation has enabled politicians to divest themselves of responsibility and, crucially, accountability for the provision of public services ... In this way, as the story of rail privatisation in Britain shows, contractors engage subcontractors and the market in services proliferates, and the provision of once public services moves out of the citizens' purview and control.

Voluntary sector or charitable organisations doing welfare work for the state, or deciding to withdraw benefits from claimants, are accountable to their own trustees. They have to reduce costs to win contracts and, as Shelter staff found out in 2008, the axe falls first on wages. The sector's ever-increasing reliance on the state has led to the creation of the National Coalition for Independent Action, which says:

> We believe there is a crisis in our ability to act independently from Government and other powerful interests, and to be part of the checks we need within our democracy. This threat to independent action will,

unless challenged, undermine our civil society, our political health, and the capacity of communities to get what they need for themselves.

An authoritarian state

Alongside this corporatisation process, the state has either shed or rendered meaningless, significant historic democratic rights. In their place has come the edifice of an authoritarian, surveillance state. Under the guise of the self-declared and spurious "war on terror", the state has:

▶ abolished the right of terror suspects to be charged within 24 hours of detention or be released and extended this to seven days in 2000
▶ further extended detention without charge to 14 and then 28 days (after failing to get 90 days). It now wants 42 days
▶ given the police blanket powers to stop, search and detain which have been used against anti-war, anti-weapons and anti-capitalist protestors
▶ created secret tribunals where people accused without charge have no right to see the evidence against them
▶ imposed indefinite detention without trial for foreign subjects which the courts later ruled illegal
▶ created house arrest without trial or evidence being presented and made this applicable to all British and foreign nationals
▶ introduced catch-all offences of "glorifying" and "encouraging" terrorism without the need to prove intent
▶ opted out of the European Convention on Human Rights on the grounds of an existing "national emergency".

The police have been given strengthened powers over citizens and as a result they can now:

▶ forcibly obtain fingerprints and other identifying features from an individual to ascertain their identity
▶ ban demonstrations or any other activity around Parliament without prior permission
▶ retain DNA samples taken from people questioned even if they are not charged
▶ intercept email and other electronic communications from internet service providers without a warrant.

The Big Brother state

The surveillance society is a society which is organised and structured using surveillance based techniques. To be under surveillance means having information about one's movements and activities recorded by technologies, on behalf of the organisations and governments that structure our society.

This information is then sorted, sifted and categorised, and used as a basis for decisions which affect our life chances. Such decisions concern our entitlement and access to benefits, work, products and services and criminal justice; our health and well-being and our movement through public and private spaces.

Everyday encounters with surveillance include:

▶ Video cameras which watch us everywhere we go – in buildings, shopping streets, roads and residential areas. Automatic systems can now recognise number plates (and increasingly faces)
▶ Electronic tags which make sure those on probation do not break their release conditions, and people arrested by police have samples of their DNA taken and kept whether they are guilty or not. 'Criminal tendencies' are identified earlier and earlier in life
▶ We are constantly asked to prove our identity, for benefits, healthcare, and so on. The UK government now plans to introduce a new system of biometric ID cards, including 'biometrics' (fingerprints and iris scans) linked to a massive database of personal information
▶ When we travel abroad, who we are, where we go and what we carry with us is checked and monitored and the details stored. Our passports are changing: computer chips carry information, and like ID cards, there are proposals for biometric passports
▶ Many schools use smart cards and even biometrics to monitor where children are, what they eat or the books they borrow from the library
▶ Our spending habits are analysed by software, and the data sold to all kinds of businesses. When we call service centres or apply for loans, insurance or mortgages, how quickly we are served and what we are offered depends on what we spend, where we live and who we are
▶ Our telephones, e-mails and internet use can be tapped and screened for key words and phrases by British and American intelligence services
▶ Our work is more and more closely monitored for performance and productivity, and even our attitudes and lifestyle outside work are increasingly scrutinised by the organisations that employ us

A Report on the Surveillance Society for the Information Commissioner, September 2006

The branch of civil law has been used to turn people, particularly teenagers, into criminals. A breach of a civil "anti-social behaviour" order becomes an imprisonable offence. Proper evidence in these cases is replaced by hearsay. The right to jury trial has been removed in complicated fraud cases and the right not to be tried twice for the same offence – the law of double jeopardy – no longer exists. Some 3,000 new criminal offences have been created since 1997. Entitlement to legal aid is now severely restricted, even in criminal cases. Under the Civil

Fortress Europe

If the British state does not feel your collar, then the burgeoning European state will. As a result of a European Union directive, local councils, health authorities and countless other public bodies will get power to access details of everyone's text, emails and Internet use. The Home Office admitted in August 2008 that it will mean companies have to store "a billion incidents of data exchange a day". The data will be made available to investigators across Europe.

EU states have turned a blind eye as the CIA has flown hundreds of prisoners through its airspace on their way to illegal torture camps - the process is euphemistically known as "rendition". The EU has bowed to American demands and intends to supply the US with information on every air passenger crossing the Atlantic. All passengers, including visitors from the USA, will be "profiled" to see if they constitute a "risk". If they are, they can be refused entry. The "profile" will be updated and held for 13 years. This will involve millions of quite innocent people being kept on record.

Tony Bunyan, *Statewatch* editor, commented: "This is yet another measure that places everyone under surveillance and makes everyone a 'suspect' without any meaningful right to know how the data is used, how it is further processed and by whom. We have already got the mandatory taking of fingerprints for passports and ID cards and the mandatory storage of telecommunications data of every communication, now we are to have the mandatory logging of all travel in and out of the EU."

Meanwhile, the Fortress Europe project is nearing completion, thanks to a new directive on the expulsion of migrants. Barrister Francis Webber says: "The idea is that there will be no hiding place anywhere in the EU for those entering or staying illegally. Wherever they go, once traced they will be liable to be removed. Someone who is ordered to leave Italy, or Spain, or Denmark, can be picked up in the UK, France or Germany and removed from the EU."

Contingencies Act 2004, the state has taken powers to allow a minister to declare a state of emergency in which assets can be seized without compensation, courts may be set up, assemblies may be banned, and people may be moved from, or held in, particular areas, all on the belief that an emergency might be about to occur. And, of course, the state is preparing for the introduction of biometric identity cards linked to databases.

The state has systematically demonised asylum seekers, denying them rights to work and to claim benefits and forcing many into destitution. Private agencies use extreme force to remove failed asylum seekers while 2,000 children annually are placed in detention, denying them their human rights. Harassed by the authorities, up to 500,000 undocumented workers have "disappeared", often working in slave-labour conditions because they have no papers.

Taken together with the illegal – in terms of international law – invasions of Iraq and Afghanistan, it is little wonder that fundamental aspects of the British state system such as the rule of law have been called into question. Helena Kennedy QC, now a member of the House of Lords, has repeatedly castigated New Labour for its attacks on civil liberties in the name of security. In her book *Just Law*, she takes New Labour to task for a "wholesale assault on the underpinnings of the rule of law". By the rule of law she means, in the area of crime for example, having clearly defined laws, access to lawyers, circumscribed police powers, an open trial process, rules of evidence, the right of appeal and the presumption of innocence. "It stands for the fundamental principle that every state actor must conform to certain basic requirements of acceptable behaviour set down not by the actor itself but by some independent body." Lord Bingham, who was until recently Britain's most senior judge, in a lecture at Cambridge University in 2006, said the rule of law meant that new laws could not overturn basic human rights. On that basis, judges had thrown out the government's detention without trial of foreign nationals because it failed to apply law to everyone equally. The fact that he devoted an entire lecture to the subject of the rule of law showed the judiciary's concern with interference by the executive and the rising scope of administrative law-making. This is also expressed in the striking down of government decisions by the courts in areas like anti-terror laws.

Growing inequality

Finally, the state has promoted inequalities on a vast scale where earlier it tried to keep these in check. So while poor asylum seekers or refugees now find it almost impossible to get into Britain, there are no such problems if you are a rich Russian oligarch or the head of a corporation. There are an estimated 250,000 Russians in London. Financial analysts say these include at least 10 billionaires and more than 1,000 millionaires who became rich by picking up privatised state industries for a song. Top of the list is Roman Abramovich, whose fortune was put at £10.6bn by the Russian magazine *Finans*. He owns a string of properties as well as Chelsea FC.

For super-rich UK residents who are not British-born, the "non-domicile" tax rule allows them to avoid paying tax on income earned overseas, which makes the UK, and London in particular, very attractive. In 2006, accountants Grant Thornton estimated that 54 UK-based billionaires were paying income tax of just £14.7m on a combined fortune of £126bn and only a tiny number paid any capital gains tax at all. The writer and broadcaster Robert Peston, in his book *Who Runs Britain?* writes:

> The triumph of the super-rich has been the most striking social phenomenon of the New Labour years. The presence on British soil of a disproportionate number of immensely wealthy people, who are becoming wealthier by the minute, has been encouraged by Tony Blair and Gordon Brown. On their watch, thanks to benign tax rules, Britain has become a billionaire's paradise. In a whole range of businesses and industries, the talent of individuals is rewarded in tens of million of pounds, while the relatively poor are getting poorer. In this jungle, where the super-predators feast best, some 30,000 people earn more than £500,000 a year, and their average income is £1.1m. They are the top 0.1pc of British earners with a combined income of £33bn, or about 4pc of all personal earnings in the UK. That is more than the value of the entire economy of Vietnam, a country with a population of 84m.

In the financial year 2005/6, a typical top 100 company boss earned 75.2 times what the typical employee was paid. And just one year's pay rise for that typical boss was £400,000, equivalent to 17 times the total pay of the typical employee.

Peston adds:

> This government has cynically exploited one of the harsh realities of globalisation, which is that millions of people on middling incomes in middling jobs do not have the clout to demand the tax reductions that the super-rich have. Only a limited number of very big businesses or stunningly talented entrepreneurs can actually up sticks to anywhere in the world, if the tax rates here are not to their liking.

Meanwhile, poverty continue to rise. One in three children in Britain live in poverty and the report *Living With Hardship 24/7* published by the Frank Buttle Trust in 2007 revealed that a quarter of the country's poorest households cannot afford to put a daily hot meal on the table for every family member. The study found that children as young as five were so keenly aware of their parents' financial difficulties that they gave back money to help support the household. The children surveyed were from 70 families across the country with an income of less than £11,000. The report's author, Dr Carol-Ann Hooper, a senior lecturer in social policy at the University of York, said:

> Children as young as five recognised that poverty was a key source of stress for their parents, and some tried to alleviate it by hiding their needs and wishes, and giving or lending money they had received from other family members. They were also often sad, angry, frustrated or upset by the impacts of poverty on their lives and hardship clearly impacted in a range of ways on all dimensions of children's well-being.

Using new ways of comparing poverty and wealth trends across Britain, a Joseph Rowntree Trust report revealed inequality to be at a 40-year high. Researchers discovered that households in already-wealthy areas have tended to become disproportionately wealthier and that many rich people live in areas segregated from the rest of society. At the same time, more households have become poor over the last 15 years. Inequality has grown sharply. In 2004, over 20% of the UK population were officially income poor compared with 13% when New Labour came to office. These figures include 3.5 million children and 3 million pensioners. Twice as many people are homeless compared to 1997. In 1996, the wealthiest 5% of the population owned 49% of wealth; by 2003 this had risen to 58%. Martin Narey, Chief Executive of Barnardo's and Chair of End Child Poverty, said:

> We are the fourth richest country in the world, we are a country where we can countenance individual bankers getting annual bonuses of £22 million while we give a family of two parents and two children, living on benefits, £10,000 to live on for a whole year.

4

The voice of the people

We have tried to show that the essential power of capitalism is concentrated in the state apparatus. Capital does not rule in a direct way; there is a division of a labour between itself and the state. This serves to mask the true, class nature of the state. This role is further obscured through the appropriation of the terms "democracy" and "freedom" by political elites in Britain whose predecessors fought tooth and nail against allowing ordinary people a say in the political life of the country.

In Britain, the owners of capital do not compel people to work for them; workers are free to choose an employer. This freedom ends at the office, shop or factory door. The state creates the conditions for capitalism to function through the enforcement of property rights. These allow for private "ownership" of capital and prevent workers from sharing in the value added through their labours. This power is implemented through enforceable rules and laws backed up by a legal system and, ultimately, physical force. The relative autonomy of the state brings its own difficulties, however. Its own power over capital is constrained. Because the state has no overall control of different branches of the economy, its capacity to act is limited. This is especially true in times of economic crisis where the state is usually more driven by events than being in control of what is taking place.

We have also demonstrated that capitalist democracy is not only limited to defined areas, but is itself being eroded under the weight of globalisation and the demands of the masters of the corporate universe. The predominant trend within the state is to authoritarian rule and the elimination of democratic rights. In a somewhat desperate bid to reclaim lost legitimacy and authority, the state has reverted to the iron fist at home and abroad. Domestically, the spurious "war on terror" claims countless innocent victims and criminalises entire communities. Abroad, the state is rampaging across the globe to try and make the world safe – not for democracy, but for the corporations and their constant appetite for new markets.

No one suggests that the oil corporations picked up the phone to Tony Blair and urged him to invade Iraq on a pretext of eliminating the fabled and non-existent weapons of mass destruction. The decision to launch a war was instinctive, and was a reflex action in response to the new economic conditions combined with Blair's desire to secure "his place in history" as a great war leader in the tradition of Churchill. The Iraqis, while they were pleased to see the back of Saddam Hussein, have not exactly welcomed the occupation of their country and the imposition of a market economy in place of the state-run, subsidised one that prevailed beforehand. Nevertheless, taken together with the war in Afghanistan, the Iraq debacle demonstrates an instability and unpredictability at the heart of the state.

At the same time, the market state is clearly incapable of applying itself to the pivotal global issue of climate change. A series of half-hearted, market-led policies like carbon credits, offsetting and nuclear power are making no impact whatsoever and probably making matters worse. What the 2006 Stern report commissioned by the Treasury called the "greatest market failure" ever is beyond the scope of the present state because action has to be directed at corporate power and its relentless expansion of production for profit.

As a result, the struggle for democracy itself, as well as the need to go beyond capitalism and the market economy to forms of co-operative and common ownership, comes directly up against the state. All roads now lead to the state and the issue of power. This is true even if actions themselves do not directly make the state itself an issue. The 2008 Climate

Camp against the building of a new coal-fired power station in Kent is a case in point. Protestors argue that coal power stations, with their high CO_2 emissions, are the most polluting means of producing electricity.

Between 1,000 and 2,000 people came to the camp over the course of a week to protest at the development of Kingsnorth. Aside from their direct protest activities, the camp also staged an extensive programme of workshop and discussion events. The state clamp down was so disproportionate that it was clearly aimed at destroying the camp. Some 1,400 officers, from 26 different forces across Britain, were brought into the area. They were supported by constant air surveillance. The Medway Ports Authority also authorised the police to "enforce" sections of their bylaws to prevent protestors approaching the power station from the river.

Around 100 people were arrested over the course of the protest, 46 of whom have been charged, mostly with obstruction offences. Riot police used batons and shields in making arrests. Section 60 of the Criminal Justice and Public Order Act was implemented to monitor and search

The powerlessness of the people

Recent episodes show how ordinary people lack power or influence when it comes to decisions at national or local level.

Invasion of Iraq. Millions marched against the planned invasion in March 2003 in the biggest mobilisation in the history of Britain. Yet the government concocted the "case for war" and imposed the decision on the country.

GM crops. The government wants to allow genetically-modified crops to be grown alongside conventional and organic crops. A consultation showed 85% of people against but the government has not dropped the plan.

Airport expansion. The government wants to build a 3rd runway at Heathrow despite widespread opposition. Independent research has exposed the government's case as deeply flawed.

Closures. Post Offices and hospitals are regularly closed without reference to the interests of local communities.

'Offshoring'. Only the shareholders are consulted when corporations relocate their business to take advantage of lower labour costs. Some workers have heard the news of redundancies through text messages.

Consultation 'farce'

Friends of the Earth announced today [7 September 2007] that it has withdrawn from the government's public consultation on nuclear power because it is seriously flawed. The consultation is also being boycotted by Greenpeace, WWF-UK, CND and the Green Alliance. Friends of the Earth's Director, Tony Juniper, said:

"This is not a genuine consultation about nuclear power. It is deeply flawed and it is clear that the government has essentially made up its mind. We are perfectly happy to debate the issue of nuclear power, but we are not prepared to take part in this latest government farce. Nuclear power is not a solution to climate change. A new programme would only generate around four per cent of the UK's energy consumption. It is expensive and dangerous, and will leave a highly toxic legacy for many generations to come.

There are lots of non-nuclear alternatives that would combat climate change, maintain energy security and keep the lights on. The government should invest in these solutions and make Britain a world leader in developing a safe and sustainable low-carbon economy. Friends of the Earth has withdrawn from the consultation for a number of reasons. These include:

▶ a lack of clear non-nuclear options which would have facilitated informed public debate
▶ a failure to provide adequate information about the wider dangers of nuclear power, such as terrorism and proliferation
▶ the `consultation' is being rushed through in five months over the summer period, and the NGO stakeholder group participation process has been rushed. The Sustainable Development Commission recommended nine months
▶ the government appears to have already made up its mind to push ahead with a new nuclear programme."

all visitors to the camp. Journalists were also searched as they entered and left the camp. The final cost of the policing operation is estimated variously between £1 million and £8 million.

On other issues, the state is simply not listening, does not care or organises fake "consultations" (see box). So it would seem that only a transformation of the state, a radical reconstruction from top to bottom of all branches of the state, can open the road to further human progress. We would agree with the Russian revolutionary leader Lenin when he wrote in his famous 1917 pamphlet *State and Revolution*:

> A democratic republic is the best possible political shell for capitalism, and, therefore, once capital has gained possession of this very best shell... it establishes its power so securely, so firmly, **that no change of persons, institutions or parties** in the bourgeois-democratic republic can shake it." [Emphasis added]

Bypassing the state

In other words, the power of capital cannot be ended without reconstituting the state. One has to admit that this remains a minority point of view, however. There are those who argue that it is possible to change society in a fundamental way without taking power and changing the state. Others in practice ignore the state, as if it were possible to change society by bypassing it. The few socialists left in New Labour still believe that the present state could somehow become a vehicle for introducing new economic structures that would undermine capitalism, even though history has shown this to be impossible.

In his 2002 book *Change the World without Taking Power*, the radical sociologist John Holloway advocates an approach that emphasises spontaneous action which somehow leads to the disappearance of capitalism without the need to replace the state. Holloway's philosophical starting point is the negativity of feelings, consciousness, and sensations, which are so powerful and important that they take precedence over the material world.

He says: "We quite consciously start from the subject, or at least from an undefined subjectivity, aware of all the problems that this implies. We start there because to start anywhere else is simply an untruth. The challenge is to develop a way of thinking that builds critically upon the initial negative standpoint, a way of understanding that negates the truth of the world." Holloway insists that what is at issue is "not who exercises power, but how to create a world based on the mutual recognition of human dignity, on the formation of social relations which are not power relations". Holloway points to the "vast area of activity directed towards changing the world in a way that does not have the state as its focus, and does not aim at gaining positions of power... "

In a review of Holloway's book for A World to Win's website, Phil Sharpe argues that Holloway wants to keep struggles at their particular, local, and spontaneous level, because automatically some greater logic of anti-power and anti-capitalism will become apparent. But while spontaneous efforts may avoid the fight for power, this very question becomes urgent if people are to change their material conditions. As Sharpe explains:

> So even when the struggle tries to be self-limiting, and restricted in scope, the spontaneous struggle will be faced with questions of power. It will be increasingly posed about how to transform a spontaneous struggle into a conscious struggle for power, because the alternative will be a serious defeat and the unrealisability of even the initial limited aims of the struggle.

Holloway's viewpoint glosses over the tendency of spontaneous movements to have alienating limitations and qualities of their own and that the tendency is to gravitate towards reformist aims and restricted trade union-type demands and the related acceptance of capitalism. Sharpe responds:

> This is why emphasis on negativity is inadequate, because it is not sufficient to oppose in practice the limits and problems of existing society. Instead the potential of negation must be consciously developed by theory and its elaboration of an alternative to capitalism as an expression of the possibilities of practice. Hence revolutionary practice cannot be automatically or objectively created out of its own logic. It requires a conscious development of unity with theory, and so practice when it is guided by theory becomes principled, consistent, and opposed to the opportunist acceptance of capitalism.

This is an extremely important point. A theory of the state, for example, is not the same as people's experiences of the state. The challenge is to unite the two in practice. Holloway's dismissal of the role of ideology in sustaining the capitalist state only serves to reinforce the status quo and offers no perspective of success. As Sharpe says: "Practice has a conscious, crucial, and dynamic theoretical aspect, and therefore theory and practice are in a dialectical unity rather than one being reduced to the other." In any case, if Holloway were even half right, and subjectivity has its required spontaneous consciousness of negativity, why has capitalism not been transcended by an ever-objectively stronger international working class?

Another important work that sidesteps the question of the state in a different way is *Empire*, by Michael Hardt and Antonio Negri. The authors have a vision of capitalism as becoming deterritorialised, and truly universal. Globalisation has replaced the nation state as the central economic and political unit of capital accumulation. There is no longer any individual, rigid and centralised power structure, but instead power is diverse and diffuse and present throughout Empire. A fluid unitary power based upon "no-space" has replaced the geographical tensions of inter-imperialist conflict. In essence, there is no state for the multitude, as they call the masses, to do battle with.

Negri and Hardt seem to suggest that the only real strategic problem is the self-repression, lack of confidence and initiative within the multitude, and if this problem is resolved then the question of political power is a historical certainty. This may seem reassuring, but it is actually an absurdity to maintain that only the repressed subjectivity of the multitude keeps Empire in control. If this were true then why haven't the multitude been able to act sooner to overthrow Empire? It is one thing to show the historical possibilities for the emergence of alternatives within capitalism, such as the subjective energy and capacity of the multitude. But it is another thing to suggest that these possibilities are effectively being realised within capitalism.

The voice of the people

There is significant evidence that a majority in Britain are in favour of political change that would give them a real say in government policies and decisions. There are also significant majorities who believe that the real power lies with the corporations and the media. Only 17% of those questioned in a 2006 survey thought that ordinary voters had a great deal or a fair amount of power over government policies. Nearly three-quarters said they only had a little power or none at all (40%). On the other hand, early eight out of ten people said they **should have** a great deal or a fair amount of power over government policies. When it came to who voters thought actually does have power over policy, the answers were clear cut. Two-thirds thought that large corporations had a great deal or a fair amount of power over the government. In other key findings, the survey established:

▶ there is overwhelming support (68%) for a written constitution, providing clear legal rules within which ministers and civil servants must operate
▶ an even higher proportion (81%), believe the Prime Minister should be bound by law to seek approval from Parliament before committing Britain to war
▶ more than three quarters believe Britain needs a Bill of Rights to protect the liberty of the individual
▶ large majorities believe that a Bill of Rights should include the right to a fair trial before a jury (89%); the right to hospital treatment on the NHS within a reasonable time (88%); and the right of a woman to have an abortion (72%)
▶ almost as many want proportional representation for elections to Westminster (60%) and local councils (62%).

The 2006 survey, for which ICM interviewed more than 2,000 people, is the seventh full-scale poll in the series. The evidence of 15 years of polls shows that the public takes a notably principled and consistent stand on democratic questions, say researchers.

In general we found that the British public is committed to the principles of accountable government, the rule of law and the separation of powers; to a renunciation of the informality of Britain's old political arrangements; to the adoption of a written constitution and strong legal and formal scrutiny of executive conduct; to more popular participation in government decision-making; and to the proportional principle in elections.

In particular, the polls over the years have shown:

▶ a strong and long established dissatisfaction with the "present system of governing Britain" (in 2004 and 2006, nearly two-thirds said that it needed "quite a lot" or a "great deal" of improvement)
▶ a five to one majority in favour of proportional representation in

In Britain, how much power would you say each of the following groups **SHOULD** have over government policies?

	A great deal	A fair amount	A little	None at all	DK
Ordinary voters	42%	36%	13%	5%	4%
The media	8%	20%	34%	29%	10%
Large companies	6%	21%	37%	24%	11%
Parliament	42%	38%	13%	4%	4%
Trade Unions	10%	31%	33%	16%	10%

In Britain, how much power would you say each of the following groups **DO** have over government policies?

	A great deal	A fair amount	A little	None at all	DK
Ordinary voters	5%	12%	34%	40%	10%
The media	28%	37%	21%	7%	7%
Large companies	29%	38%	17%	6%	9%
Parliament	53%	27%	10%	4%	6%
Trade Unions	18%	36%	28%	7%	11%

State of the Nation 2006 survey. Joseph Rowntree Foundation

elections to Parliament and local councils in 2006

▶ growing public sympathy for most popular protests in recent years, with high levels of people in 2004 agreeing that the destruction of GM crops, petrol blockades and refusals by pensioners to pay council tax were justified.

The researchers conclude:

It is in civil society that the great strength of democracy in Britain lies. The Rowntree polls demonstrate that the citizenry active in voluntary societies and action, trade unions, tenants and trade associations, non-governmental bodies such as the Child Poverty Action Group, Christian Aid, the Countryside Alliance, Liberty, Oxfam, the Royal Society for the Protection of Birds, and a host of protest, sports and community groups, draw much of their strength from a public that might well be uninformed, but nevertheless demonstrates a normative sense of the importance of principles of democracy and social justice in British political life.

Similar conclusions were reached by the Power Inquiry, which was set up to discover what had happened to the political system and why "disengagement from formal democratic politics in Britain [has] grown in recent years and how can it be reversed?" The commission, chaired by radical lawyer Helena Kennedy QC, reported in 2006 that it was "vital to re-engage the British people with formal democracy" if the following are to be avoided:

▶ the weakening of the mandate and legitimacy for elected governments – whichever party is in power – because of plummeting turnout
▶ the further weakening of political equality because whole sections of the community feel estranged from politics
▶ the weakening of effective dialogue between governed and governors
▶ the weakening of effective recruitment into politics
▶ the rise of undemocratic political forces
▶ the rise of a "quiet authoritarianism" within government.

The final report insisted that the British public are not apathetic, adding:

Very large numbers of citizens are engaged in community and charity work outside of politics. There is also clear evidence that involvement in pressure politics – such as signing petitions, supporting consumer boycotts, joining campaign groups – has been growing significantly for many years. In addition, research shows that interest in 'political issues' is high.

The area of decline is in formal politics: turnout for general elections has declined very significantly since 1997; turnout for other elections has remained stubbornly low for years; party membership and allegiance has declined very severely over the last thirty years; elected representatives are held in very low esteem and widely distrusted.

Turnout plummets

▶ turnout in both national and local elections has fallen dramatically in the last decade – the 2001 and 2005 elections recorded the lowest turnout (59 and 61% respectively) since the advent of universal suffrage in 1918

▶ while in 1970 there was an 18 point difference between the 18-24 age group turnout rate and the 65-74 age group rate, by 2005 the gap was 40 points

▶ 75% of people aged 65 and up voted in the last election compared to only 37% of young people. In other words, for every two older people who voted in the last general election, only one younger person voted

▶ although there has been some decline in turnout among all income categories since 1964, the decline is most rapid for those in lower income groups. Moreover, whereas turnout increased in 2005 among better-off groups, it continued to fall among low earners

▶ turnout at local elections has fallen by around a tenth since the 1980s, with the result that little more than a third of registered electors turnout to vote in most local elections

▶ turnout tends to be lowest in poor inner city areas where there is a high proportion of young people. Typically only about 80% of the population are registered to vote in these areas, and even in national elections only around 40-50% of those registered turn out to vote.

A Citizen's Duty, Institute for Public Policy Research, May 2006

The commission's own research and experience established that the level of alienation felt towards politicians, the main political parties and the key institutions of the political system is extremely high and widespread. The inquiry found that the following explanations stood up in the face of the evidence:

▶ citizens do not feel that the processes of formal democracy offer them enough influence over political decisions – this includes party members who feel they have no say in policy-making and are increasingly disaffected

▶ the main political parties are widely perceived to be too similar and lacking in principle

▶ the electoral system is widely perceived as leading to unequal and wasted votes

▶ political parties and elections require citizens to commit to too

broad a range of policies
- ▶ many people feel they lack information or knowledge about formal politics
- ▶ voting procedures are regarded by some as inconvenient and unattractive.

In the end, the Power Inquiry could not, of course, think beyond the existing political system or consider why it might be inherently undemocratic. Its aim was to bring voters back into the fold by "rebalancing" the system of power. Ironically, it was Helena Kennedy herself who had berated New Labour for "rebalancing" the justice system in order to erode basic liberties and defendants' rights. So the first group of the inquiry's 30 recommendations were aimed at allowing "the freedom for our elected representatives to be the eyes, ears and mouths of British citizens at the heart of government". They demanded a concordat between the executive and Parliament "indicating where key powers lie and providing significant powers of scrutiny and initiation for Parliament". The recommendations to give select committees real power, to place limits on the powers of the whips (who control how MPs vote), to give Parliament powers to initiate legislation, to decentralise power to local government, to "map" quangos and their powers and to keep a register of ministers' meetings with lobbyists hardly begin to answer the issues the inquiry itself established.

The second group of recommendations were designed to develop an electoral and party system which is "responsive to the changing values and demands of today's population" and covered proportional representation, reducing the voting age, a cap on donations to political parties and state funding to support local activity. Hardly radical let alone revolutionary thinking, considering the political system is in deep crisis. The final group of recommendations aim to create a "culture of political engagement" with direct input into policy and decision-making. These covered giving citizens the right to demand inquiries and hearings into public bodies and their management, changes in the way the media functions and the holding of annual general meetings by MPs. Unfortunately, taken separately or together, the Power Inquiry's recommendations fail to raise the political temperature and, in some cases, are naïve. They fail to address the nature of the state and how power is actually exercised.

The real conclusion is that the parliamentary state has outlived its usefulness and is actually a barrier to maintaining democracy let alone enhancing it in new ways. The surveys reported in this chapter indicate a real desire for change and for power over policies and government. As a result, the mass of people are effectively disenfranchised, unrepresented, and remain alienated from the state that rules over their lives. It makes them prey to reactionary populists, nationalists and the far right who make claims to represent ordinary people's thwarted aspirations.

No one should be surprised at the lack of response in official circles, apart from the odd dose of lip-service to democracy and "engaging" with people. There are boundaries and limits beyond which the state cannot go. Once formal, representative democracy was established, the capitalist state has proved remarkably resistant to going any further in a meaningful way. In practice, it cannot do so and no amount of pressure, protest, petitions, policy proposals, reform ideas and so on will alter this reality. Proposals that potentially undermine the authority of the existing state will be resisted. States throughout history have always done the same. No state will give up its power voluntarily.

This is even more true of the present state because in the last analysis it is a proxy state, ruling on behalf of corporate and financial power. Its duties and responsibilities are ultimately not to the mass of the people, the electorate, but to a narrow group of elites. Their particular power is in itself more diffuse than ever in the context of globalisation. Any threat to state structures runs the risk of leading on to a general transfer of power, in economic as well as political terms, to the mass of the people. Not only will such threats be countered, they will be met with the coercive powers of the state if the need arises and answered with force. That being the case, how are we to expand the scope of democracy beyond its present limits?

5

A way forward

The state remains the lynchpin of the social system of capitalism, holding it all together. It provides the essential ideological, political, social, legal, educational and coercive frameworks without which society in general and capitalism in particular cannot function. Therefore, the state – who controls it, the way it is organised and in whose interests – is our main political focus.

Transformed by the march of global capitalism, the state is unable and unwilling to uphold or sustain the democratic forms that have allowed it to rule over the majority. Without new democratic forms, it is inconceivable that we could reorganise the economy along not-for-profit lines, put an end to war and act on the ecological crisis. Without a comprehensive revolutionary regime change we cannot breathe new life into democratic achievements and make the right to vote mean something again.

Representative democracy was a great step forward in the historic struggle for rights. It enabled working people to build independent political parties like the Labour Party and win significant reforms through the parliamentary process. But that period of history has drawn to a close with the emergence of a market state, marked in Britain by the transformation of Labour into capitalist New Labour. The state has lost its legitimacy and authority by:

▶ merging its identity more closely with corporate interests
▶ devolving more and more power to unelected, unaccountable bodies
▶ taking away long-established democratic rights
▶ using state violence and war in a bid to enhance its role
▶ trampling all over the rule of law at home and internationally
▶ creating unparalleled inequalities of wealth and opportunity
▶ targeting the poor, migrants and the youth
▶ refusing to meet social needs like housing and care in older age
▶ proving incapable of tackling climate change and other major challenges.

The existing parliamentary system is a façade that increasingly undermines and devalues the right to vote that was won in bitter struggle against the ruling classes. A single vote every four or five years in a general election cannot alter the fact that this form of democracy is limited and curtailed in so many ways that reform is impossible. We should, instead, see the achievement of representative democracy as a stepping stone to greater things. There is unfinished business to complete.

Extending and expanding democracy to express the power and rule of the people has to focus on building a momentum which leads to the dismantling of the existing state. In its place, the people themselves would develop a transitional state that takes forward the achievements of the last 200 years in winning basic democratic rights. This would be achieved by breaking down the very real limits to democracy imposed by the capitalist system. It would go beyond representative democracy, which actually dilutes and filters the aspirations of the powerless majority until they are acceptable. Abolishing the artificial distinction between political and economic power would create the conditions for the rule of the majority for the first time in history. Instead of being the handmaidens for other classes to assume power, as they have been in the past, ordinary people can achieve power for themselves.

We have demonstrated why the existing state structures cannot become the servant of the people and that neither protest nor pressure can induce substantial change. That is why the governmental, administrative, judicial and repressive apparatus of the capitalist state has got to go. As part of this agenda, Britain's currently neutered Parliament could be transformed into a body with real executive power as part of a democratic state at all levels in society. A people's convention on the constitution could extend democracy in new ways:

▶ **Co-ownership of resources.** The key areas of the production and financial process, including land, would transfer from private shareholder ownership into forms of co-ownership. These resources would be held in trust by locally-elected bodies and placed under democratic control.

▶ **The workplace.** All workers should have the right to democracy at work, whether in a factory, hospital call centre, in public transport, civil service, local government, offices, shops, schools, colleges or university. All major decisions would require the consent of the workforce. Self-management would be encouraged in place of hierarchies.

▶ **Education.** Students at secondary and higher levels should get the right to take part in the running of their institutions.

Our proposals are aimed at creating the conditions where the state as a special body alienated from society begins to disappear, where it becomes unnecessary. The first step along this road is achieving state power, with the purpose of abolishing what is oppressive, secretive and unnecessary, and reordering the remainder so that it serves the interests of the majority. The principles for a transitional state should include:

▶ self-organisation throughout society where possible
▶ involving as many people as possible in government and administration
▶ an end to special privileges and incomes for state officials
▶ total accountability and subordination of all officials to elected bodies
▶ elections for all public offices
▶ complete transparency and openness at all levels
▶ new legal and justice systems based on community control and self-policing.

Alongside democratic ownership and control of economic and financial resources, we should build on the formal democratic rights we have achieved and give them real meaning and content through a new political framework. This would rejuvenate the House of Commons, and would mean the abolition of the totally unelected House of Lords, monarchy and the secretive Privy Council, A framework for a new democratic Britain could be built around:

- ▶ local and regional People's Conventions with executive as well as deliberative power and control over resources in place of existing local government and other structures
- ▶ delegates to reflect diversity in our communities, with distinct voices for women, minority ethnic citizens, older people, young people, workplaces, students and small businesses
- ▶ an electoral system in balance with the new participatory system
- ▶ local and regional People's Conventions to decide on how best to meet a range of needs in their own areas and to send delegates to a national Convention/Parliament with law-making powers
- ▶ all matters discussed, debated and decided upon with full public access
- ▶ delegates to be paid no more than the average national income
- ▶ all delegates subject to recall and removal by local/regional voters at any time
- ▶ mass involvement in the new democratic process through the Internet
- ▶ extensive consultation with voters *before* decisions are taken at any level
- ▶ freedom of political representation and the right to organise politically.

Democratic rights

Today, individual rights to justice, like the ability to elect for trial by jury, are under constant attack by the state. We need to restate them in a fresh way. Individual rights to liberty and freedom from arbitrary arrest will be reaffirmed in unconditional and positive terms in a Bill of Rights. There will be explicit rights to:

- ▶ *Habeas Corpus,* requiring people arrested to be brought to court and charged or released immediately

- free and equal legal representation
- freedom from state surveillance and interception of communications
- inspect freely all data held by the state and other bodies
- organise, associate, demonstrate and strike independently of the state
- for minority communities to equality in all areas
- for the free movement of people based on "no borders" principles.

Economic and social rights

Economic and social rights are disregarded by the British state. A new constitution would enshrine enforceable rights in a charter. They should include:

- decent housing at affordable cost for everyone
- free education for students at all ages; The right to free continuing education and training
- employment for those who can work and average pay for those who cannot
- the right to co-operative ownership and self-management
- the right to democracy in all areas/activities of the workplace
- equal pay and job opportunities for women; free child care for single parents
- free health care at all levels and types of treatment
- dignity in old age through pension provision at average income, and free care
- safe and nutritious food at affordable prices
- the right to live in an environment shaped by ecological care and basic human needs
- the right of nature, including human beings, to exist free from abuse and despoliation
- affordable access to cultural and personal development opportunities
- the right of communities to continuity of culture, traditions and habitat.

Law and the legal system

The legal system in Britain, although it is an inseparable part of the state machine, fulfils a number of often contradictory roles. It can, for example, often come into conflict with other parts of the state and government. We have seen a number of examples of this, both under the Tories and New Labour, where the judiciary has argued for the protection of democratic rights and the rule of law. At one level, the legal system – with its judges, courts, lawyers and prisons – is clearly an expression of the dominant power relations and ideology in society. It is based on hierarchy, authority and the ability to deprive those who do not "obey the law" of their liberty and the ability of those with money to buy the best lawyers. These are all expressions of the power of the state. The judiciary sits as representatives of the "Crown" – which in 21st century Britain means the state and not the monarchy.

Much – but not all – law in Britain is handed down by the state in the form of legislation. Lawyers are accredited by bodies that owe their powers to the state. Prisons lock people up on behalf of the "Crown", which is why they are known as Her Majesty's Prisons. From this standpoint, the legal system has no essential independence from the capitalist state. The legal system upholds private ownership of property and contract law as the cornerstone of capitalist society. But because the ruling classes do not rule in a direct fashion, the legal system has developed a relative autonomy. The legal system in Britain thus reflects within it both the dominant nature of capitalist rule and the struggle for rights against arbitrary state power that stretches back many centuries.

Because the democratic achievements of society as a whole are enshrined in the legal system, albeit in a contradictory way, the transition to a new kind of state must necessarily involve struggles over law and constitutional issues. Under circumstances of major social conflict, legal issues can acquire a revolutionary dimension. As E.P. Thompson has noted, (foreshadowed by philosophers like Hobbes and Spinoza) the rule of law is a cultural achievement of society as a whole. It does not benefit the ruling classes alone. In times of crisis, the defence of law can provide a focus for a revolutionary transfer of power.

Our proposals

We need to take forward what human society has achieved in terms of law while rejecting the existing class-biased framework in favour of a revolutionary, new approach. Law must guard against corruption of the new democratic society by bureaucrats, political opportunists and other interests. Previous achievements should form the basis of a new framework for law that goes beyond the limitations set by capitalist social relations.

▶ the rule of law must embrace published laws that apply universally, laws that are never retrospective, freedom from arbitrary arrest and defined limits to the powers of the state
▶ if law is to serve society as a whole, all links between the legal system and the state must be severed
▶ judges must be allowed to judge on the basis of the law alone and not some overriding principles set down by the state
▶ the selection of judges at all levels must be a transparent process free from interference by the state and involve judges, lawyers and ordinary people, who would get special training to help them in their task
▶ judges must reflect regional, social and economic groups in society. Lay judges should sit alongside professionals
▶ a special commission would investigate what laws inherited from capitalism need scrapping or amending in the light of the framework of the new society.

Crime and punishment

The most evident class bias in the legal system is in the area of crime. Laws setting out offences all derive from legislation drawn up by the state and imposed on the legal system to implement. The concepts of individual responsibility, guilt and punishment that lie at the heart of criminal law express both the hostility of the state and the atomisation of the individual in capitalist society.

The criminal law system is not so much about "justice" or even "fighting crime" as a way of reinforcing existing punitive forms of social control and authority. For example, prosecuting a company for manslaughter is next to impossible. The intense exploitation of workers in Britain and abroad, which shortens lives and makes people ill, is not considered a crime. While terrorist bombings are dealt with as crimes, the dropping of bombs on civilians by state-employed pilots is legally sanctioned. Undercover police who killed Brazilian electrician Jean Charles de Menezes in July 2005 faced no charges. Carbon emissions are destroying the planet's ecosystems and making people ill, yet those responsible are not considered criminals.

The rapid changes of the last 35 years have shattered many of the forms of social relations that developed after 1945 in the period of economic boom and the welfare state. Market forces have produced far less stable households, urban degeneration, the growth of extreme wealth alongside deprivation, the marginalisation of sections of young people, burgeoning individualism, and a manufactured craving for consumer goods.

The decline of informal social control through relatively stable communities has coincided with the dramatic fall in the price of drugs to produce whole inner-city as well as rural areas of decline and despair. Young men, in particular, have seen their traditional status and social role challenged and this has deepened their alienation. Increasing numbers of young women have struggled against the odds as lone parents. This is the background to contemporary crime, much of which is committed by the poor against the poor. The courts deal harshly with offenders while the rehabilitation aspects of the system are downgraded.

Statistics provided by the Prison Reform Trust speak for themselves:

▶ on 16 May 2008, the prison population in England and Wales was 82,682. In France, with a similar sized population, the figure is 56,279

▶ England and Wales has the highest imprisonment rate in western Europe at 147 per 100,000 of the population

▶ in December 2007 the government announced an additional 10,500 prison places to be built by 2014. This is on top of the existing 9,500 capacity programme

▶ the number of prisoners in England and Wales increased by 25,000 in the ten years from 1996 to 2006. Previously it took nearly four decades (1958-95) for the prison population to rise by 25,000

▶ total prisons expenditure has increased from £2.8bn in 1995 to £4.3bn in 2006 (all at 2006 prices)

Solutions lie outside prison bars

There are differing ways to respond to clear, up-to-date information about the state of our prisons and the state of people in them. One is to see relentlessly rising prison numbers, coupled with unacceptably high reconviction rates, as a storage problem and to respond by commissioning a £6billion warehouse building programme designed to increase prison capacity to over 100,000 places by 2014.

Another is to use what is known about the men, women and children in prison, and the offences for which they are being held, to ask fundamental questions about the purpose of imprisonment, and its social and economic outcomes, and to act to introduce proportionality into sentencing, invest in effective community penalties and to call on a range of government departments to shoulder their responsibilities for increasing well being and reducing offending...

Investment instead in treatment for addicts would lead to a measurable drop in offending. Much acquisitive crime, shoplifting and theft, is driven by drugs. Binge drinking fuels violence and public disorder offences. In a welcome move government has commissioned Lord Bradley's review of the scope for diverting the mentally ill and people with learning disabilities from police stations and courts into much-needed health and social care. The fact is so many of the solutions to crime lie outside prison bars.

Prison Reform Trust, June 2008

▶ the number of women in prison has nearly doubled over the past decade to 4,500 in May 2008. More than 17,700 children are separated from their mother by imprisonment

▶ at the end of March 2008 there were 2,350 children in prison

▶ it costs an average of £40,992 to keep a person in prison in England and Wales

▶ a 22% increase in the prison population since 1997 is estimated to have reduced crime by around 5% during a period when overall crime fell by 30%

▶ 64.7% of offenders are reconvicted within two years of being released – for young men (18-20) it is 75.3%.

Our proposals

These horrific statistics shows the urgent need to reframe the whole concept of crime and how to deal with it. With the abolition of the alienated social relations of capitalism, communities will have greater opportunities to explore what defines crime from a totally different standpoint. Instead of naming and shaming, retribution, vengeance and punishment, we should:

▶ emphasise reparation and community self-control and influence
▶ replace the body of existing criminal law, with its thousands of offences, with law based on making offenders face up to their responsibilities and their impact on communities
▶ scrap the existing, barbaric prison system. Where it is unavoidable to detain offenders, a new approach would make rehabilitation its sole priority
▶ formal court structures that presently deal with crime could be replaced with neighbourhood/community courts that would start from compensation and reconciliation rather than retribution and revenge
▶ decriminalise drugs as a step towards dealing with the abuse issue
▶ increase the use of arbitration, adjudication and conciliation so that communities come to accept that they have a responsibility for the personal and social development of all of their citizens.

The police and the secret state

The police force in Britain is incapable of serving communities because of the way it is established, run and controlled. Created originally to enforce the decisions and property foundations of the capitalist state, the police are alienated from the communities they claim to serve. At times of social crisis, the police are deployed to protect the state and the authorities. In most recent history, the police were used by the Thatcher government to attack miners and print workers in the mass struggles in defence of jobs that took place during 1984-6. They also violently suppressed the anti-poll tax demonstrations in London in April 1990. In addition, the police Special Branch works closely with MI5, the British secret police, to spy on and infiltrate those considered to be a "threat to national security". This goes far beyond the alleged terror networks, to militant trade unions, leftwing political organisations and protest groups opposed to government policy.

At another level, the police are clearly incapable of dealing with crime. The bureaucratic, secret world of the police means they are often closer to the criminal fraternity than ordinary people. In fact, often their behaviour mimics aspects of the most backward social behaviour in the shape of racism, corruption, indifference and lying when it comes to obtaining convictions. As a result, many vulnerable and innocent people end up serving long sentences for crimes they did not commit.

There is a secret face of the state – the state within the state – which has a virtual free hand to act against what it perceives as the "enemy within", to borrow a phrase used by Margaret Thatcher to describe the miners' leaders during the epic 1984-5 strike for jobs. The methods used by the secret state range from surveillance, both physical and electronic, to the infiltration of agents into movements and the deployment of *agents provocateurs* to encourage acts of violence/law-breaking in order to make arrests. There are murky bodies such as the Research, Information and Communication Unit which specialise in disinformation and planting stories in the BBC and other media.

During the 1970s, sections of the MI5 secret police actively plotted against the Wilson governments. Sections of the army also colluded with media magnates and establishment figures in plans for a military-led coup during the oil crisis and miners' strikes of 1973-4. In the north of Ireland, special forces and intelligence agencies carried out illegal assassinations and fed information to Loyalist forces. More recently, during the build-up to the Iraq war, the part of the state that operates in the shadows helped to concoct "evidence" to justify an invasion.

If the official state is not spying on you, privatised spooks almost certainly will be. According to research by Stephen Armstrong (*New Statesman*, 7 August 2008), private espionage is a "booming industry" and environmental protest groups are its prime target. He cites Russell Corn, managing director of Diligence, one of a growing number of "corporate intelligence agencies", who told him: "If you stuck an intercept up near one of those camps, you wouldn't believe the amount of outgoing calls after every meeting saying, 'Tomorrow we're going to cut the fence.' Easily one in four of the people there are taking the corporate shilling."

Data interception

Leading human rights groups in Ireland and the United Kingdom in 2008 secured a victory before the European Court of Human Rights over data interception. The Irish Council for Civil Liberties (ICCL), Liberty and British-Irish Rights Watch took their case to Strasbourg because, over a seven year period, all telephone, fax, e-mail and data communications between the UK and Ireland, including legally privileged and confidential information, were intercepted and stored en masse by an electronic test facility operated by the British Ministry of Defence.

Finally, the European secret state is at it as well. Proposals made in 2008 by the shadowy "Future Group" set up by the Council of the European Union include a range of measures including new technologies of surveillance, enhanced cooperation with the United States and harnessing the "digital tsunami". In the words of the EU Council presidency: "Every object the individual uses, every transaction they make and almost everywhere they go will create a detailed digital record. This will generate a wealth of information for public security organisations, and create huge opportunities for more effective and productive public security efforts."

Our proposals

The community should learn to police itself, relying on professional help where necessary. That would require the abolition of the police force as presently constituted and its reorganisation to support community self-policing. The secret intelligence agencies, MI5 and MI6, together with the police Special Branch would also be abolished. The army,

Paris commune

Abolishing the bureaucracy at once, everywhere and completely, is out of the question. It is a utopia. But to smash the old bureaucratic machine at once and to begin immediately to construct a new one that will make possible the gradual abolition of all bureaucracy – this is not a utopia, it is the experience of the [Paris] Commune, the direct and immediate task of the revolutionary proletariat.

V.I. Lenin, *The State and Revolution*. Moscow 1917

together with the navy and air force, which is used to fight wars on behalf of the capitalist state, would be reorganised as a defensive force as a prelude to their dissolution. All their weapons of mass destruction will be scrapped.

State administration

The state administrative machine is composed of departments, executive agencies and quangos. It is inherently conservative and remote. Expertise is used to reinforce the status quo and vested interests. Existing government departments function to maintain social control. For example, 90% of those involved in carrying out the functions of the Home Office are attached to the prisons and asylum systems. The Ministry of Defence spends billions on armaments to use against other countries, or to sell to poor nations where rulers deploy British-made weapons to keep their own populations down. Other ministries openly promote business interests.

Our proposals

We will be obliged to replace the existing administrative machinery. In its place would come new bodies that are totally under the sway and control of national, regional and local People's Assemblies. For example, a new department concerned with trade would encourage self-management in the workplace, help create an audit of productive resources, stimulate ideas about new technology with the purpose of reducing workloads and cutting working hours and turn scientific research institutes away from commercial priorities in favour of solving pressing problems facing society.

Furthermore, all departments would devolve not just staff but also their functions, to regions and cities to help ensure that bureaucratic inertia does not dominate. As far as state administration is concerned, the principles for the future could be:

- ▶ the subordination of bureaucracy to society through accountability to Assemblies
- ▶ the elimination of state administration wherever possible
- ▶ an end to special privileges and making a career out of bureaucracy

▶ payment of staff to reflect general levels of incomes in society

▶ complete public transparency in the work of the bureaucracy.

Conclusion

A World to Win is confident that by making information technology available to everyone, by bringing the economy under the control of communities, workers and consumers, and by discouraging bureaucratic trends wherever possible, the state as a separate body can eventually be dispensed with. When the class divide is ended by abolishing the power of capital over people's lives, the need for a state will start to evaporate. That is why we are advocating a *transitional state*. As society develops in a co-operative way, a state machine whose purpose is to administer people will no longer be necessary. The more that people get involved in determining their own lives in collaboration with others, the more diminished will be the power of the state and the more unnecessary it will become.

The changes outlined here amount to a revolution in thinking as well as practice. They emphasise not only the continuity of the struggle for democracy but also the leaps in history that are required to open up new eras. To date, the result of the struggle for power within capitalism has always resulted in new minorities seizing control of the state while making use of the strength of the masses to attain their objectives. Our objective is the transfer of power to the majority, which the development of society itself has made possible. The majority, in any case, actually keep society functioning whether they work in the state, offices, schools, shops, hospitals, factories, call centres or in financial services. It is about encouraging working people to become conscious of their own potential as much as anything else.

In any case, many functions of the state have themselves been simplified or eliminated under globalisation. The corporations have developed tremendous productive capacity, enough to meet need in every country, while demonstrating that it is possible to run large-scale enterprises without managerial bureaucracies. These are crucial differences by comparison with the Russia of 1917, when the Russian Revolution overthrew the capitalist state but started from a low cultural level and a predominantly peasant economy. Unable to break out of an imposed isolation, the revolution ultimately degenerated and the democratic sprit of early Soviet power was buried by a bureaucratic, tyrannical Stalinist state. Our circumstances are far more positive and encouraging.

No one can forecast exactly how such a transfer of state power would take place. While the contesting of elections is important as a way of raising the issues discussed in this book, the limitations of this approach are clear. The state can tolerate elections because they do not present a threat to actual power. Where fundamental social change is posed, history indicates that a mass, revolutionary movement with a leadership prepared to stay the course and complete the task is absolutely indispensable.

The opportunities for success are favourable. The capitalist state is in a weakened condition after exhausting the period of representative rule. Representative democracy has turned into its opposite – unrepresentative oligarchy. Moving to authoritarian rule becomes the state's Achilles' heel.

By demonstrating ever-diminishing control over events like climate chaos while clearly lacking popular support, the capitalist state presents itself as the barrier to future human progress. History needs to move down another, democratic path to a popular state where self-determination of people is the mainspring. Achieving this transformation of power will simultaneously open up the possibilities of moving beyond the limiting nation-state system towards a world federation where people's national identities can sit harmoniously alongside one another. Crucial to succeeding in this project is the ability of groups like A World to Win and others to extend their influence, showing how seemingly disparate struggles for rights can find their lasting solution in the struggle for democratic power itself.